Trophies, Relics and Curios?

Sidestone Press

Trophies, Relics and Curios?

Missionary Heritage from Africa and the Pacific

edited by

Karen Jacobs
Chantal Knowles
& Chris Wingfield

Published by Sidestone Press, Leiden
www.sidestone.com

ISBN 978-90-8890-271-0

Lay-out & cover design: Sidestone Press
Photograph cover: Tolai Mask, New Britain, collected by Rev. George Brown. h. 76 cm, accession number Oc1986,03.1. Courtesy of the Trustees of the British Museum.

This publication is an outcome of the networking research project *Who Cares? The material heritage of British missions in Africa and the Pacific, and its future*. Funded by the Arts and Humanities Research Council (grant number AH/J008494/1), the project was led by Dr Karen Jacobs, Sainsbury Research Unit, University of East Anglia, and Dr Chris Wingfield, Museum of Archaeology and Anthropology, University of Cambridge, with Chantal Knowles of the National Museums Scotland as a project partner alongside the Museum Ethnographers Group.

Contents

Introduction

Karen Jacobs and Chris Wingfield

Over the past two centuries, a majority of the people living in and around the Pacific Ocean and across the landmass of sub-Saharan Africa have become adherents of Christianity, in its various forms. Whatever one thinks about the desirability of this change, its significance, in global historical terms, is staggering. While there has been a recent profusion of independent and Pentecostal churches in these parts of the world, which have been the subject of a great deal of scholarly attention (eg. Anderson 2013; Miller, Sargeant and Flory 2013), it is undeniable that the roots of many African and Pacific churches lie in the protestant missionary movement which developed in Britain at the end of the eighteenth century, and took advantage of the opportunities offered by an expanding empire (Cox 2008). By concentrating on a range of artefacts, material things made by humans, which have survived from the British Protestant missionary movement over the last two centuries, this book attempts to cast light on the multiple historical events and exchanges which together made up this movement.

At one level, the artefacts, whether museum collections, memorials or historic churches, themselves constitute missionary heritage – they have been inherited from a past to which missionary endeavour contributed considerably. At another level, however, heritage is less about the things themselves, and more about how we deal with them and negotiate their significance in the present. Through focussing on a diverse range of artefacts, this book aims to draw out these questions of significance, and explore the different ways in which artefacts with origins in the missionary past may be important for different communities in the present. These groups include contemporary Christians in Africa and the Pacific, people from these parts of the world living in Europe, but also Europeans themselves.

While mission histories loom large in shaping both landscapes and identities in much of sub-Saharan Africa and the Pacific, where the architectural remains of early missions are frequently recognised as significant heritage sites, they are more easily forgotten in Europe. In Britain, apart from a small number of memorials and blue plaques on buildings associated with famous British missionaries (most notably

Figure 1. View inside the main room of the London Missionary Society (LMS) museum, printed in the *Illustrated London News*, 1843. Note the model Tswana house to the left of the giraffe, shot in 1813 by LMS missionary John Campbell's party in the Northern Cape. The model house features in Elliott's chapter, the giraffe in Wingfield's chapter. *Illustrated London News*, 20 May 1843, page 342. Courtesy of Chris Wingfield.

David Livingstone), the most significant material reminders of overseas missionary activity are collections of portable material, brought and sent back to Britain by missionaries. Many are kept today in small and large museums across the British Isles. It is fair to say that in many cases their connection to the British missionary movement is often unknown and largely unacknowledged. In larger collections, such as those of the British Museum or the Pitt Rivers Museum in Oxford, many of these artefacts are presented primarily as ethnographic specimens, examples of things made in Africa or the Pacific, without significant acknowledgement of the complex histories of religious conversion and encounter from which they originate.

Reassessing the significance of these objects in the light of these histories, however, means considering a period before the category of ethnographic object was in widespread use (see Kirshenblatt-Gimblett 1991). The terms more usually applied to such artefacts when they arrived in Britain were those used in the title of this book: trophies, relics and curios. One example of this usage comes from a pamphlet produced in 1908 to introduce *The Orient in London*, the largest missionary exhibition ever organised by the London Missionary Society (LMS), at London's Agricultural Hall, at the time one of the largest exhibition spaces in the world:

> *Innumerable courts are furnished with curios and trophies, with treasures rich and rare, telling here of a martyr missionary's last bold venture, there of an intrepid explorer's plunge into some land where white men's feet had never trod, and on every side objects illustrating the emergence by barbarous nations from the habits and customs of darkness into the splendours of a civilisation ennobled by love.... Ten thousand stewards, all specially trained and primed with the requisite knowledge, will explain the objects exhibited in the Courts, make the foreign scenes realities, give life to the relics and shed romance round the trophies.*[1]

The aims of this volume are rather more tentative than those expressed for the 1908 exhibition. We are nevertheless interested in exploring a world in which such exhibitions took place, and in which the use of these three terms in such an unselfconscious way was possible. They are all terms with a long history, predating the development of the British missionary movement, but it is significant in each case that this was the terminology that came to hand most readily to describe the objects that emerged from missionary encounters. They are terms that are rather infrequently applied to artefacts today, but their relative unfamiliarity makes them useful categories through which to explore the different ways in which particular artefacts gained significance in the past, but also the ways in which they continue to be relevant to people's lives today.

The division of the chapters of this book into these three categories is intended to explore their relevance, but also to question their applicability. Each term implies a particular form of significance, whether recalling remarkable achievements in the case of trophy, as remnants of noteworthy people and events in the case of relic,

---

1 *The Orient in London. A Great Missionary exhibition*, Agricultural Hall, June 4 to July 11 1908. Pamphlet held at the Council for World Mission archive (CWM/LMS. Home. Miscellaneous (Odds). Box 31), SOAS, London.

or simply suggesting the curiosity that arises from encountering the unfamiliar, in the case of curio. By using a question mark alongside these terms we intend to question whether the complex histories that surround each of the artefacts, explored in the individual chapters of this book, can readily be covered by a single categorisation. Many of the artefacts could equally have featured under a different category, suggesting that a rigidly imposed categorisation would be unhelpful since artefacts frequently assume multiple significances over the course of their biographies.

Nevertheless, we intend to explore the categories of trophy, relic and curio as artefacts in their own right – human concepts with origins in particular historical contexts, which were picked up and reused in others. Part of the reason for this must be that they retained a use value – they express a particular way of engaging with things which is not entirely context dependent, and has echoes and resonances in other times and places, much like many of the artefacts described in particular chapters. The precise significances of these terms developed in missionary contexts over time, and for this reason, among others, the chapters in each section of this book are ordered in approximate chronological order. Although not central to what individual authors set out to convey, some sense of the shifting significance of these terms can be gained by reading the chapters in each section in order.

Trophies?

The word 'trophy' has its origins in the Ancient Greek term *tropaion*. Early *tropaia* were erected to mark the place where a turning point occurred, usually in a battle. These consisted of captured weapons and armour of the defeated enemy hung from the branch of a tree. In later periods they were also erected at ceremonial sites such as Olympia and Delphi where more people might see them and in the Roman period, *tropaia* were also erected in Rome itself. In later periods, the *tropaeum* – a figure formed from armour and shields – became a sculptural decoration that adorned more prominent architectural markers of military victory such as Trajan's column in the forum at Rome (Davies 1997, 42).

We are perhaps more familiar with the term today from a sporting context, where gilded cups and plates are presented to the victors of sporting contests and competitions, but this contemporary use of the word shares with its ancient origins a strong human drive to mark moments of significant achievement in material form. A photograph of a sporting victor embracing their trophy is more eloquent on the front cover of a newspaper than the extended textual narration of the victory that follows.

British missionaries, particularly during the nineteenth century, were not immune from this trophy-taking instinct. The stuffed giraffe that stood at the centre of the LMS museum for much of the nineteenth century (Figure 1), and discussed in Wingfield's chapter, has the appearance of a straightforward hunting trophy. While it was given to the missionary traveller John Campbell, rather than shot by him, it nevertheless became a trophy of his travels beyond the colonial frontier of South Africa in 1813, ultimately featuring on the frontispiece of the published account of his travels. Nevertheless, Campbell's giraffe was progressively upstaged, and ultimately displaced by another sort of trophy, far more connected with missionary endeavours than the specimens of natural history that he collected (Wingfield 2012a).

This shift in focus for the LMS museum was initiated by an event in 1816, discussed in Maia Nuku's chapter. The decision by the Tahitian chief Pomare II to send his 'family idols' to London refocused missionary collecting practices towards 'idols' as missionary trophies par excellence. Objects associated with non-Christian religious practices, particularly when given up on the point of conversion by their owners became important markers of missionary success, and ultimately reminders of these significant events. While 'idols' were displayed and sometimes even paraded at church meetings in Britain, they were also widely depicted, frequently to accompany textual accounts of the events from which they arose. They were also sometimes subjected to acts of inscription, through which missionary ownership and control over them was asserted (Jacobs 2014).

Nevertheless, Nuku suggests that the intentions underlying the presentation of such items by the original owners to missionaries were complex. These probably owed a great deal to pre-existing understandings of the capacity for potent artefacts to cement relationships through acts of exchange. In addition, Andrew Mills' chapter suggests that acts of conversion, and the presentations of artefacts to missionaries that followed them, sometimes emerged from worlds of immense political complexity. Missionaries, he suggests, were sometimes the pawns rather than the players in complex political and military stratagems, deployed by local leaders primarily against their rivals. In such contexts, it seems likely that missionaries frequently mistook for acts of faith, the specific political significances that the exposure and presentation of the objects they regarded as 'idols' had for their local audiences.

By the mid-nineteenth century, the humble supporters of overseas missions in Britain could themselves acquire trophies of missionary activity through the sales that were organised by missionary societies. In his chapter, Steven Hooper focuses on an image from the Illustrated London News of an "Exhibition and Sale" organised by the Wesleyan Missionary Society in 1851. He points out that presentations of items to missionaries by local converts in Fiji, which built on a range of pre-existing practices, rapidly acquired an equivalent status to the offerings left in church collection plates in Britain, as items were efficiently converted by missionary societies into cash through fundraising activities such as missionary sales.

During the second half of the nineteenth century, individual missionaries increasingly supplied collected objects directly to the many civic museums that emerged in the wake of the Great Exhibition of 1851. In her chapter on "Livingstone's loom", Sarah Worden points out that David Livingstone, like John Campbell before him, made a fairly eclectic collection of material during his African journeys. Nevertheless, the loom that he presented to the Industrial Museum in Edinburgh, from what is now Malawi, emerges as an item of particular significance for several reasons. Firstly it resonates strongly with Livingstone's own biography, with his early years spent working in an industrial cotton mill on the river Clyde. The loom was presumably significant for Livingstone both as a familiar technology and as an indicator of labour and industry. In addition, Worden points out that the loom resonates with more recent efforts to revive hand weaving in Malawi as a craft skill.

Joshua Bell's chapter, like Wingfield's, focuses on a natural history specimen – a Moustached Treeswift from Papua New Guinea – but demonstrates how missionary collecting networks, which included local teachers, overlapped with and contributed to the scientific networks that developed during the nineteenth century. Nevertheless, the collecting of specimens for the emerging science of anthropology in the later nineteenth century still sometimes had a great deal in common with missionary trophy collecting of the earlier nineteenth century. In her chapter on an Efate drum from Vanuatu, donated to the museum in Edinburgh by the Scottish Presbyterian missionary James Lawrie, Chantal Knowles suggests that missionaries continued to understand these drums as religious statues and their removal as an important marker of conversion. Similarly, the complicated status of a "sorceror's kit" from Papua New Guinea, as both a scientific specimen and a missionary trophy, is explored in Tabitha Cadbury's chapter, where it seems clear that its collector Harry Moore Dauncey was both extremely interested in understanding sorcery practices, but at the same time personally committed to their eradication.

The relationship between anthropology and missions is given a further twist in Rachel Hand's chapter about a brass necklet at the Museum of Archaeology & Anthropology in Cambridge. While it was presented through the missionary anthropologist John Roscoe, it was actually given by Apolo Kaggwa, the Katikkiro (prime minister) of Buganda in the British Protectorate of Uganda, a Christian convert who seems to have actively facilitated and directed much of Roscoe's anthropological work, including the collecting of a range of ritually and ceremonially significant items. Hand speculates about whether for Kaggwa, it was actually the University of Cambridge, and his involvement with it, that became the trophy in this case.

Ben Burt begins his chapter on a carved wooden bird at the British Museum by asking why its missionary collector, Arthur Hopkins, did not record more detail about its original significance. He outlines the complicated circumstances that surrounded Hopkins' presence in north Malaita, Solomon Islands, and shows that his relationship with a local Chief, Kaialafa, was central to this. Hopkins' autobiography suggests that the presentation of this carving to Hopkins by Kaialafa marked a real turning point in their relationship, suggesting that it functioned not as a trophy of conversion, but of acceptance and friendship.

The interview with Kanak archaeologist François Wadra by Julie Adams, which ends this section, draws out some of the contemporary significances that items, collected by missionaries as trophies, continue to have in the Loyalty Islands. Wadra suggests that despite their absence, the histories of many of the most notable items are still known, and their ongoing potency poses a set of complex issues for him when he encounters them in European museums. For Wadra, despite their removal to Europe, the spirit of these objects has remained in the islands from which they came.

Nevertheless, the heritage of missionary encounters is not straightforward for Wadra, some of whose ancestors themselves became missionaries. Depicted in this chapter is a monument erected on Maré, Wadra's home island, to commemorate the arrival of missionaries from the London Missionary Society, a marking of space that has much in common with the ancient Greek *tropaia*. Wadra also points out that people on Maré retain a section of the canoe in which the first Polynesian missionaries arrived, as a relic of this significant event.

Relics?

While the relics of heroes were preserved in sanctuaries in Ancient Greece, including famously the ship of Theseus, the term 'relic' is more readily associated with the practices of medieval Christianity. In early Christianity, the physical remains and possessions of saints, and particularly martyrs, were especially venerated, associated with a sense that departed saints might intercede on behalf of the living. The significance of these practices appears to have grown over time and the Second Council of Nicaea in 787AD decreed that every Christian altar should contain a relic. In the Medieval period, a widespread trade in relics emerged, and alongside it a significant traffic in pilgrims who travelled to sites that preserved the relics of saints, such as Santiago de Compostela in Spain (Bagnoli, Holger and Mann, 2010).

Figure 2. Image of the Relics display at the Orient in London exhibition, 1908. Images of famous missionaries such as John Williams and Robert Moffat were shown alongside objects associated with them during their lives. Courtesy and Copyright Council for World Mission / SOAS (CWM: Home/Photos/Box 2 File 10A).

Nevertheless, the theological significance of relics became controversial and contested, and a rejection of the significance of relics formed one element of the Protestant Reformation in Europe during the sixteenth century (Koerner 2004). It is strange then that British Protestant Missionary Societies of the nineteenth and twentieth centuries should use the term relic at all.

However, it appears that many supporters of mission felt a sense of veneration and awe for certain missionaries (and especially those who were martyred in the course of their work) that approached the way in which saints and martyrs were viewed in the early church. A section of the *Orient in London* exhibition, referred to above, even went under the title 'Relics', and it was here that items associated with famous LMS missionaries such as David Livingstone, John Williams, Robert Morrison and James Chalmers were displayed (see Figure 2). The David Livingstone Memorial, created at his birthplace in Blantyre, Scotland, became a location at which relics from Livingstone's life were gathered, and was even imagined as a future site of pilgrimage on its opening in 1929 (Wingfield 2012b, 125).

One such item that continues to be preserved at Blantyre is "David Livingstone's Magic Lantern", described in T. Jack Thompson's chapter. This was used by Livingstone as a means of evangelization during his voyages into the interior of Africa, and evidently made an impression on those who encountered it. Nevertheless, Thompson makes clear that Livingstone was keen to explain how it worked, in order to dispel any sense of magic that may have surrounded people's initial encounters with it. Preserved and presumably collected because of its association with a famous missionary, the magic lantern nevertheless speaks of the importance of this mode of presentation for communicating missionary ideas to audiences in both Africa and Europe.

A combination of different kinds of significance is also explored in Steven Hooper's chapter in this section, discussing a wooden image from Fiji which recently fetched a high price at auction in Paris. While this may have originally functioned as an ancestor image (a relic of a sort), it seems likely to have been regarded as a trophy by its missionary collector Thomas Baker. Nevertheless, Hooper suggests that one reason for its economic value today is its association with Baker, the only European missionary to have been killed in Fiji. The martyrdom of Baker in 1867 is also central to the chapter by Sagale Buadromo and Katrina Talei Igglesden, who describe the display in the Fiji Museum of the remains of Baker's shoes, donated by the Methodist Church of Fiji & Rotuma in 1873. This chapter suggests that such relics continue to be significant foci for attempts to work through the troubling inheritances that such events continue to have in the present. The juxtaposition of these relics in the museum with objects associated with pre-Christian practices, and still regarded with suspicion by many Christian Fijians, underlines the sense of potency with which such objects continue to be imbued in the Pacific.

Ben Wate's chapter on the relics of Bishop John Coleridge Patteson, preserved in St Barnabas Cathedral in Solomon Islands, also concern the remains of a missionary martyr. However, Wate suggests that Bishop Patteson's memory is equally preserved through a number of intangible practices. These include the regular narration of the story of his death, an annual festival of remembrance, but also the naming of children after a man now regarded as a heroic ancestor figure by many Christians in Melanesia – a contrast with his position in Britain, where he is almost forgotten today.

Jill Hasell's chapter explores the Tolai mask from New Britain that features on the front cover of this book. Its acquisition by the British Museum in 1986, a century after it was originally collected, occurred in the context of the sale of the larger collection made by the Methodist missionary George Brown to the National Museum of Ethnology in Japan. Hasell suggests that the export licence for this item was withheld partly because of its rarity, but also because there was some recognition of the importance for British history and heritage of George Brown's role as a missionary in the western Pacific. Today, the mask can be regarded as a relic of the larger collection of which it formed a part, but also of George Brown himself, a somewhat controversial figure who enacted revenge on Tolai people following their killing of Fijian missionaries in 1878.

In his chapter, Paul Lane considers not a portable relic, but the remains of the "African Church", built to hold a thousand worshippers at Old Palapye in the early 1890s. Today a gazetted National Monument in Botswana, the original building of this church was financed by Chief Khama of the Bangwato, who also supported the establishment of the Livingstone memorial in Blantyre. Nevertheless, Lane suggests that the church should not simply be regarded as a relic and symbol of Bangwato commitment to Christianity, but that its subsequent abandonment can also serve as a reminder of the sometimes strained relationships that emerged between European missionaries and African leaders as they attempted to reshape spiritual and cultural landscapes together.

Wingfield's chapter in this section considers a bell from the headquarters of the LMS in London, where it served as a relic of the *SS John Williams*, a missionary ship in the Pacific between 1893 and 1930. In a complex way, however, the ship itself, and network of connection it created between different Pacific Islands can be regarded as relics of the missionary John Williams, after whom the ship was named. Williams became known as the "Martyr of Erromango" following his death there in 1839, and honouring his memory became a major focus of missionary fundraising during the nineteenth century. However, the ramifications of his death continue to be felt today, and Carol Mayer's chapter considers a green dress that was presented to her as a participant in a reconciliation ceremony that took place in Erromango with the descendants of John Williams in 2009.

The violent deaths of certain missionaries, while sometimes celebrated in Europe as acts of martyrdom, also frequently fed into discourses about the inherent barbarism and savagery of Africans and Pacific Islanders, which found a particular focus in the idea of cannibalism. These connected issues are central to a work by the Samoan artist Greg Semu: *The Last Cannibal Supper… cause tomorrow we become Christians*. In an interview with Jacqueline Charles-Rault, which ends this section of this book, Semu reflects on the creation of this work, which refers particularly to Leonardo Da Vinci's depiction of "The last supper". Semu's work draws attention to the contradictions and complexities of missionary encounters, in which consumption of the flesh of defeated enemies was replaced by the metaphoric consumption of the flesh of a divine saviour, in the form of the Eucharist.

Curios?

If the word 'trophy' is associated most strongly with the Ancient World and 'relic' with the Middle Ages, the term 'curio' is an altogether more recent creation. The word came into use during the mid-nineteenth century as an abbreviation of the term 'curiosity', which itself had a fairly long history of use. Nevertheless, 'curio' was a value-laden term which expressed a rather dismissive attitude towards the items it was used to describe. It has been suggested that the term curio was a pejorative term indicating a lowly status and relative insignificance (MacClancy 1988: 163).

This is perhaps in contrast to the associations and usages of the unabbreviated term 'curiosity'. In general, this was used to refer to things that were unusual, strange, or peculiar and therefore generated a form of curiosity and wonder from those who encountered them. Cabinets of curiosities – *Wunderkammer* – were rooms filled with eclectic and encyclopaedic collections of objects that proliferated across Europe during the sixteenth and seventeenth centuries. In many ways a precursor of later public museums, the *Wunderkammer* of this period mingled natural and artificial wonders, conceptually and often physically, united in their capacity to generate wonder. Displays were intended to encourage comparisons, through analogies and parallels – creating an encyclopaedic perspective (Jefferson and Robinson 1995, 44).[2]

It is these twinned associations, a connotation with marvel and wonder on the one hand, and the subsequent condemnatory subtext of the term 'curio' on the other, which lends a particular significance to the term when considering items associated with the British missionary movement. Items that may have been unremarkable 'curios' in their day have in some cases become significantly more curious with the passage of time, as the circumstances from which they arose have receded into history. In using the term here, accompanied by a question mark, we want to question the pejorative sense in which it may have been applied to such items in the past, and suggest instead that they may emerge as objects of real interest, from which a great deal can be learnt through sustained engagement and study.

One of the central arguments of this book is that missionary encounters were far from straightforward or singular – multiple parties were involved in influencing their outcomes, and in shaping the artefacts that resulted from these encounters. Local people influenced the collection of trophies and participated in the creation and curation of relics. The 'Curios?' section of this book concentrates on items which materialise these complex encounters, indeed, things that were often generated by missionary encounters themselves.

---

2 See also Arnold 2006; Impey and MacGregor 2001; Kenseth 1991.

Catherine Elliott Weinberg begins this section with a focus on a scale model of a nineteenth century Tswana house, made by LMS missionary Robert Moffat and displayed in the London Missionary Society museum. Rather curiously it was reported as a New Zealand Maori house in an 1830 illustration, revealing how intertwined and confused European notions of Africa and the Pacific could become at this time.

In another case of mistaken identity, Jacobs considers a wooden doll at the Fiji Museum, dressed in Fijian clothing and once assumed to have been produced by Fijian craftsmen. Recent research has suggested that it is a Grodnertal doll, made in Austria and shipped abroad to be dressed in local clothing. Ironically, the doll was owned by a missionary family active in Fiji between 1839 and 1845, who were themselves involved in persuading Fijian people to abandon the traditional styles of dress that the doll bears witness to. It is ambiguities and complex interconnected histories such as this, which emerge from the close examination of objects that may once have been dismissed as mere curios.

Anita Herle examines a drum which at first sight appears to be a traditionally manufactured item from the Torres Strait. However, the chapter reveals the ways in which it incorporates a number of innovative modes of design and decoration which express the complex relations that developed between Saibai Islanders, the London Missionary Society, and Samuel McFarlane, the missionary to whom it was presented just before he returned to Britain.

As well as collecting items in Africa and the Pacific that they took to Europe, missionaries were heavily implicated in the movement of goods in the opposite direction. Ceri Ashley considers an item that was discovered at a mission site in northern Botswana during recent archaeological excavations. The chess piece in question appears, at first sight, straightforwardly European, but it is suggested that the curiosity of the chess piece arises partly because it represents a materialisation of missionary ideals relating to the rational use of leisure time, but also because it can be read as a symbol of the isolation and challenging conditions at the Lake Ngami Mission, which led to its abandonment after just three years.

Another peculiarly European artefact, transplanted abroad through the establishment of overseas missions, are the communion tokens from Vanuatu, discussed by Eve Haddow. Although inscribed in the Efate language, these tokens have their roots in practices that arose in Scotland during the reformation of the sixteenth century, but travelled to the Pacific with Scottish Presbyterian missionaries. Although the items she discusses come from museum collections, Haddow raises the intriguing possibility that further examples might be discovered during archaeological investigations currently being undertaken in Vanuatu.

Jocelyne Dudding's somewhat archaeological reading of a photograph of a woman suckling a child, taken in the Congo by the Baptist Missionary Kenred Smith, is extremely suggestive of the negotiations that must have taken place between the missionary photographer and the woman he depicted. This chapter also draws attentions to the negotiations and resistances that took place between Kenred Smith and Anatole von Hügel, the Cambridge curator who was keen to acquire his photographs, but equally anxious where possible to exclude signs of missionary presence, such as the wearing of European clothing and cloth.

In his chapter, Nick Stanley asks what terminology we should use to describe an item that is on display at Birmingham Museum where it is presented as a 'communion cup' from the Solomon Islands. While made of local material and according to local techniques, it is more likely to have been sold as a curio rather than actually used. Is it helpful to think of this as a 'syncretic object' or are we on safer grounds referring to it simply as a 'curio', which is probably how it was described at the time it was made? Our working definition for the category of curio has been objects that cannot be explained by reference to pre-existing cultural practices in Africa, the Pacific or Europe, alone, but emerge from the cross fertilisation of these different worlds.

This category has enabled us to discuss things that are curious in the sense that they are anomalous, defying straightforward cultural classifications. One such item is the parade knife, discussed by Johanna Zetterstrom-Sharp and originally collected by the Baptist Missionary Lionel West in the Belgian Congo during the mid-twentieth century. Adapted from an earlier form, the knife features a figure with its arm raised in what appears to be a salute. Through its complex meshing of different forms and motifs of decoration, this object appears to materialise large-scale transformations in social and political life, which witnessed the establishment of a new religion alongside the emerging centrality of military force in Central Africa.

A widespread conception of the missionary enterprise, at least in Europe, is that it involved the suppression of local cultural practices. The artefacts in this section of the book, however, suggest that in many parts of the world, missionary encounters also provided opportunities for extraordinary moments of cultural creativity, spawning a wide range of new cultural and artefactual forms. The interview with the artist Atta Kwami that ends this section explores his own family's engagement with the opportunities offered by (German) missionaries to the Volta region of Ghana, culminating in the artistic practice of his mother Grace Kwami. Emerging from the interview as something of a curio, at least according to our definition, is Atta Kwami's artist book, *Grace Kwami Sculpture*, a tribute to his mother's life and work. The book form, which captures the importance for Protestant missionaries of the written word, nevertheless takes the shape of a spider, associated with the figure of Kweku Ananse in Ghana, denoting ingenuity and skill.

Engaging Missionary Heritage in the Present

Taken together, the items explored in the 'curios' section, and indeed in the book as a whole, suggest that missionary encounters, and the artefacts that have emerged from them, involved a range of complex negotiations, and a great deal of 'give and take'. While the terms applied to objects, 'trophy, relic and curio', have longer-term European antecedents, the ways in which these terms were deployed in missionary contexts was equally shaped by circumstances that arose from beyond Europe. New forms of cultural practice emerged in Europe as a result

Figure 3. Façade of the Papua New Guinea Parliament in Port Moresby. Photograph by Joshua A. Bell, 2002.

of missionary encounters, just as they did in Africa and the Pacific. However, far from this 'proliferation of hybrids' necessarily resulting on conditions of peaceful coexistence, it has also given rise to recurrent projects of 'purification', to use the language of Bruno Latour (1993).

In 2013, devout Christian Theodore Zurenuoc, the speaker of Papua New Guinea's national parliament, damaged a lintel of nineteen ornately carved heads from the iconic façade of Parliament House as he considered them 'ungodly images and idols' (Eves and Hayley 2014: 1). The Parliament House in Papua New Guinea (PNG) opened in 1984 as a symbol of the country's future as a free nation after it gained independence from Australia in 1975. Evoking the shape of an East Sepik province *haus tambaran* (spirit house) and including other indigenous cultural expressions, the building aimed to express the nation's unity as inclusive of cultural diversity. However, in 2013 the building became the centre of controversy when the parliamentary speaker, with the support from Pentecostal churches, appeared to condemn the carvings as an embodiment of demonic power and a spiritual threat to the nation. Zurenuoc's actions allow a wide range of interpretations and are not merely a result of his endeavour to redefine PNG's national identity in Christian terms. His actions have also been interpreted as resulting from PNG's problematic amalgamation of church and state and the country's close relationship with Israel in terms of its foreign policy.[3] As complex as it is, this recent example can nevertheless be considered as a form of missionary heritage that is not unparalled elsewhere. Not only does it demonstrate the ongoing consequences of mission work in the Pacific, it also emphasises the material dimensions of religious conversion and missionary encounters that we have sought to underline in this volume. While the example might involve the destruction of traditional expressions – something that was also a significant feature of many missionary encounters – the large number of churches in African and Pacific landscapes, African and Pacific objects in museums, as well as the range of artistic expressions inspired by Christianity and Christian imagery, express the fact that missionary encounters were not simply destructive, but at times also immensely creative.

The missionary past is one that binds Europe to Africa and the Pacific, and is therefore a past that underlies and informs ongoing relationships in the present. Whether in museums, archaeological sites or archives, the material heritage of British overseas missions is of significant interest to a range of global stakeholders. The same objects can provide scholars with evidence of complex histories of global exchange, and indigenous cultural activists with rare evidence of pre-Christian cultural and religious practices. Objects removed by missionaries as evidence of paganism and idolatry can remain objects of suspicion for contemporary Christians at the same time as western scholars regard them as masterpieces of 'world art'. Through associations with particular named missionaries, items can even acquire the emotional charge of 'relics'. However, for non-specialist curators in regional British museums, the primary significance of such material may appear to be its associations with particular locally based missionaries. This makes it all the more important to draw attention to the potential for this material to have globally significant associations, since British missionaries were amongst the earliest and certainly most socially integrated Europeans in many African and Pacific communities.

A crucial feature of missionary heritage is thus its potential to become a focus for reflections on shared histories by people from different parts of the world, with the attendant ambiguities and complexities that this involves. Rather than present missionary encounters as the outcomes of purely western agendas, we hope that the various chapters of this book together use the material heritage of British overseas missions in Africa and the Pacific to address and demonstrate the multiple values and valuations that can be brought to this connected set of material resources, from a diverse range of different perspectives.

Acknowledgments

This publication is an outcome of the project *Who Cares? The material heritage of British Missions in Africa and the Pacific, and its future*, funded through a networking grant from the UK Arts and Humanities Research Council (grant number AH/J008494/1). The project was established as a partnership between the Sainsbury Research Unit at the University of East Anglia, the Museum of Archaeology and

3 For more information on the case study, see Eves, *et al.* 2014; Schram 2014.

Anthropology at the University of Cambridge, and National Museums Scotland, Edinburgh, which each hosted a workshop, and the Museum Ethnographers Group, which hosted a webpage for the project.[4] This research network primarily addressed the stewardship of cultural heritage for future generations, and was concerned with the complexities that emerge around material generated by the overseas engagements of British missionary societies in Africa and the Pacific (see Jacobs and Wingfield 2014). During the first workshop, the core group of participants each introduced themselves and their research by showing an image that represented their engagement with missionary heritage. The diverse variety of perspectives which emerged is, we hope, reflected in this publication. We would like to thank all workshop participants, keynote speakers and contributors for their stimulating insights and engaging discussions. Finally we would like to thank Jenny Reddish for her invaluable help.

4 See http://www.museumethnographersgroup.org.uk/en/projects/330-ahrc-network.html

Part One

Trophies?

FRONTISPIECE.

Drawn by the Rev.d W. T. Strutt. Engraved by H. Meyer.

The Author of Travels to South Africa, with waggons &c. on the Banks of the Great or Orange River.

Giraffe, South Africa

Chris Wingfield

At sunset on 31 July 1813, John Campbell (1766–1840) heard the sound of musket-shots. The Minister of Kingsland Independent Chapel in London, Campbell had departed for South Africa in June 1812 as a representative of the directors of the Missionary Society, as the London Missionary Society was then known. His brief was:

> *... personally to inspect the different settlements, and to establish such regulations... as might be most conducive to the attainment of the great end proposed – the conversion of the heathen, keeping in view at the same time the promotion of their civilization.* (Campbell 1815, viii)

Having recently returned from an arduous six week journey by ox wagon to Lattakoo (Dithakong), a Tswana town in the north, Campbell had spent most of the day writing letters back to England (Campbell 1815, 346). He was staying at Klaar Water, a settlement north of the formal frontier of the Cape Colony, where missionaries from his society had been working for much of the previous decade. Campbell was in the process of persuading the people who lived there to stop referring to themselves as Bastards, or Hottentot Bastards, on account of "the offensiveness of the word to an English or Dutch ear" (Campbell 1815, 349).

Shortly after Campbell heard the shots, a messenger arrived to tell him that "a camel-leopard had been shot and they wished me to see it before it died" (Campbell 1815, 346). Although he hurried, Campbell found the giraffe collapsed, but was nevertheless astonished at the length of its fore legs, "nearly six feet, so that a high horse could have walked under his belly" (Campbell 1815, 346). No doubt impressed by Campbell's reaction, the person who shot the giraffe presented him with its skin "to carry to England" (Campbell 1815, 346). At a meeting the following week, the male residents of Klaar Water agreed to adopt a code of laws and system of justice, to refer to themselves as Griqua, and to rename their settlement Griqua Town. They also decided to name their satellite settlement, 48km to the east, Campbell in his honour.

Figure 1. Frontispiece, published in Campbell's (1815) Travels in South Africa, showing him in Africa, with a giraffe in the background. Courtesy and Copyright of Cadbury Research Library: Special Collections, University of Birmingham.

Campbell arrived back in Plymouth in May 1814, and immediately began speaking and preaching about his journey. Early the following year he published an account of his journey: *Travels in South Africa Undertaken at the Request of the Missionary Society* (Campbell 1815). The frontispiece of this (Figure 1) shows its diminutive author sheltering from the African sun under a dark umbrella. A caption printed in the book referred to the "waggons &c" pictured "on the Banks of the Great or Orange River". While the landscape, and particularly the oxen, appears somewhat European, there is one element of the image that suggests Campbell must be in Africa – the giraffe grazing on a tree in the background.

Following Campbell's return to London, the giraffe's skin, along with a number of others, was prepared for display by the London taxidermist Benjamin Leadbeater (Seton 2012, 98), and it was presumably from this mounted version that the image of the giraffe on the frontispiece of Campbell's book was created. The return of Campbell, accompanied by various hunting trophies from his travels, appears to be one of the main reasons why in the succeeding months the Missionary Society decided to take some rooms "in which the curiosities sent by our missionaries may be deposited" (Lovett 1899, 91). From April 1815, visitors to the Missionary Society's rooms in central London could encounter the giraffe face-to-face at full standing height. *A Guide to London*, published in 1817, noted that the curiosities on display were "mostly from Africa and the South Sea islands", and that "many persons viewing these are induced to become subscribers to the fund" (Hughson 1817, 68-9).

Campbell departed for a return journey to South Africa in November 1818, shortly after the arrival in London of the "family gods" of Pomare the "King of Otaheite" in September of that year (see Nuku, this volume).[5] Campbell returned to London in May 1821 with a number of additional specimens of natural history, including the skull and horns of a rhino, but it is clear that animals such as the giraffe, which later catalogues of the LMS museum referred to as "Specimens in Natural History", were increasingly eclipsed by the interest shown in "Various Idols of Heathen Nations".[6]

Nevertheless, Campbell's giraffe stood at the centre of the LMS Museum for many decades, despite a number of relocations. In 1823, the Museum moved to Austin Friars, and the catalogue published in 1826 describes the giraffe, or *camelopardalis*, at the centre of the room:

> *This very peculiar animal inhabits the interior parts of Africa, and the forests of Ethiopia. It is remarkable for the great disproportion of height between the fore and hind parts. The head is like that of a Stag; the neck is slender; the tail long, with strong hairs at the end; the whole is of a dirty white, marked with large broad rusty spots.* (LMS 1826, 15)

5 "Otaheite", *Evangelical Magazine and Missionary Chronicle*, February 1818, 81.
6 "Frontispiece", *Catalogue of the Missionary Museum*, Austin Friars, W. Phillips: London, 1826.

This catalogue description goes on to refer to the depiction of giraffes by the Romans in the Praenestine Pavement. The LMS Museum moved again in 1835, to Blomfield Street, and the earliest known depiction of the museum, from 1843, also shows the giraffe at the centre of the room (see Introduction Figure 1).[7] However, its dominant height was now challenged by the Rarotongan staff god, which arrived from the Pacific in 1834. In a way, this represents the gradual shift of the LMS museum from an institution dominated by specimens of African natural history towards one that became dominated by "IDOLS AND OBJECTS OF SUPERSTITIOUS REGARD", mainly from the Pacific, but also India and China (LMS n.d., 5). An 1843 description of the museum concentrated on the "the numerous idols and articles of heathenism", noting enthusiastically that the museum contained "upwards of three hundred gods", only mentioning Campbell's giraffe towards its end (Campbell 1843, 135-6).

The giraffe remained at the centre of the LMS Museum, with its head projecting into the space of the skylight well into the 1850s, although other specimens of natural history are much less apparent in an image of the museum that appeared in the *Lady's Newspaper* in April 1853.[8] In 1859 a further image in the *Illustrated London News* showed the recently rearranged interior of the museum, with the giraffe no longer apparent.[9] A catalogue which appears to match the arrangement in this image lists the giraffe, but only at its end, surrounded by other specimens of natural history which seem to have been removed to another room (LMS n.d., 51-2).

In 1878, a short item in the *Evangelical Museum and Missionary Chronicle* noted that the LMS museum had been relocated from the "the midst of the back land" to a newly built upper floor in the main building, where it was "carefully arranged in the new cases provided for it".[10] While this refers to the "especially rich" collection of "South Sea Idols", no mention is made of the Giraffe or the other natural history specimens, and it is unclear whether they were removed from the museum altogether at this stage, since the ultimate fate of Campbell's giraffe remains unknown. Following the centenary of the foundation of the LMS in 1895, it became clear that the "relics and trophies of a hundred years' war with barbarism and superstition" (Gordon 1899, 88) did not include the preserved remains of various African animals, even though these had filled the LMS museum when it was established in 1814.

7 "Missionary Museum", *Illustrated London News*, 20 May 1843, 342.
8 "Museum of the London Missionary Society", *The Lady's Newspaper*, no. 326,16 April 1853, 237.
9 "The Museum of the London Missionary Society", *Illustrated London News*, 15 June 1859, 605.
10 "The London Mission House", *Evangelical Magazine and Missionary Chronicle*, January 1878, 10.

THE FAMILY IDOLS OF POMARE,

Which he relinquished, and sent to the Missionaries at Eimeo, either to be burnt, or sent to the Society.

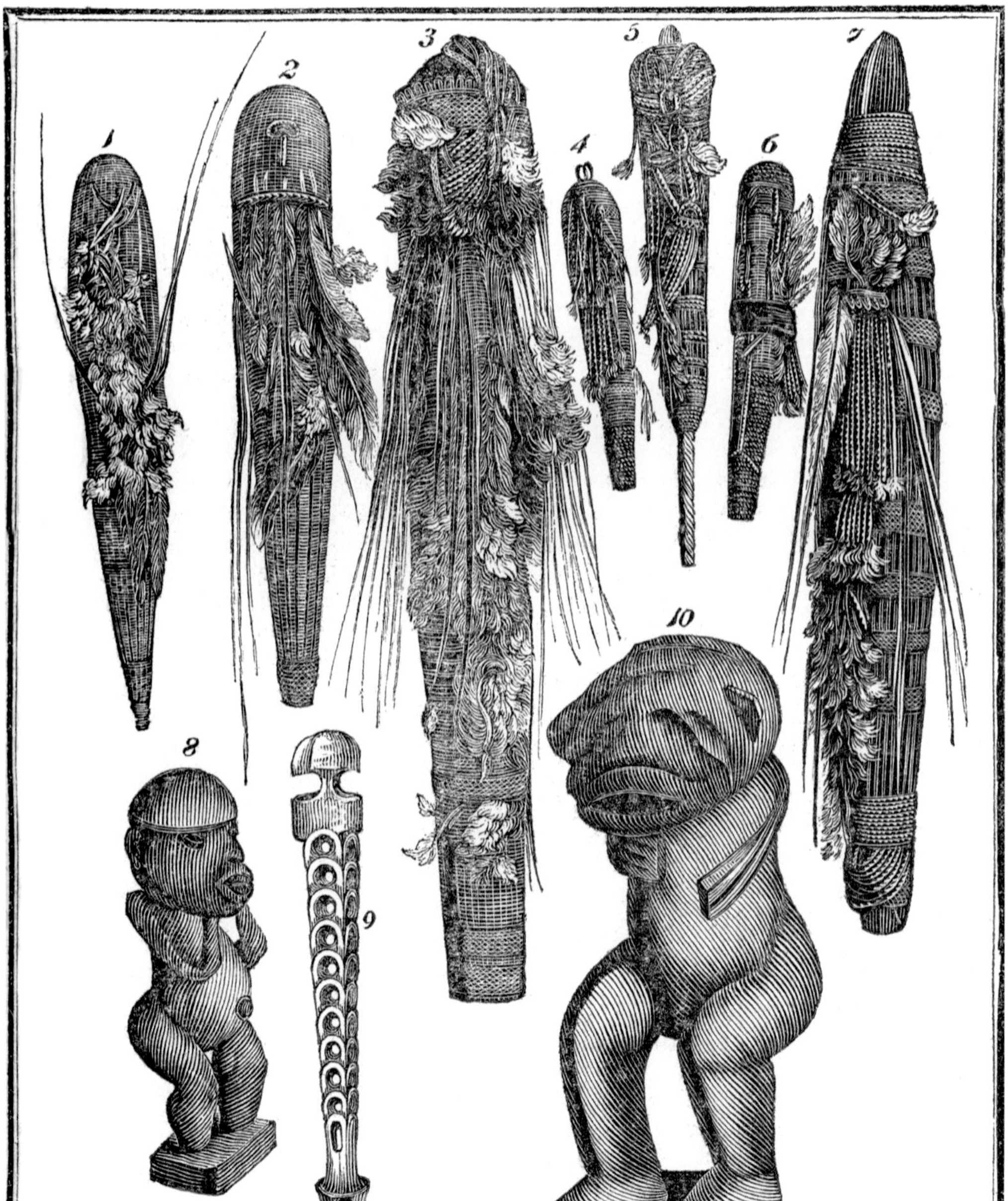

The Family Idols of Pomare, Tahiti, French Polynesia

Maia Nuku

The decision of Tahitian chief Pomare II to dispatch a first consignment of idols to London in 1816 was a pivotal moment in the history of the London Missionary Society. Two decades of interaction with missionaries had finally led Pomare II to test the new religion. Certainly the period of early missionary encounter in Tahiti had been an extremely volatile one. The increased confidence of the Pomare dynasty, and in particular Pomare II's ambitions to increase his secular authority by consolidating his position as *ari'i rahi*, paramount chief of the islands, had met with strong resistance from neighbouring district chiefs. From the outset the Pomares had proved themselves particularly innovative in their dealings with Europeans, actively pursuing strategies of engagement which aimed at incorporating visitors into existing networks to assert their authority to the best political advantage.

Stretching the privileges associated with their sacred status as the descendants of gods, the Pomares developed a well-established strategy to promote their links to the cult deity Oro in bold and visual ways, not least in their assertion of rights to the possession of the dramatic ritual paraphernalia associated with his worship – namely the *maro 'ura*, *taumata* and *to'o*, complex feather- and sinnet-bound waistbands, headdresses and god images, the latter of which will be discussed in more detail below. Intensified ritual activity placed great demands on an already strained population and the period saw existing hostilities frequently erupt into open warfare as loyalties shifted and political realignments were forced. Existing tensions and uncertainties were further exacerbated by the severe disruption caused by famine and disease. This had created an environment in which islanders now questioned the efficacy of their own gods and, faced with the possibility that these were no longer delivering, the material and spiritual benefits of Christianity began to seem like a proposition worth entertaining.

Pomare II forwarded a selection of his household gods to missionaries in the settlement at Papetoai on Mo'orea with an accompanying letter, dated Feb 1816, in which he explained his motives:

Figure 1. The Family Idols of Pomare, Missionary Sketches III (October 1818). Council for World Mission archive, SOAS Library, CWML L50.

Friends ... I wish you to send those idols to Britane for the Missionary Society, that they may know the likeness of the gods that Tahiti worshipped ... If you think proper, you may burn them all in the fire; or, if you like, send them to your country, for the inspection of the people of Europe, that they may satisfy their curiosity, and know Tahiti's foolish gods! (*Missionary Sketches III*, October 1818, 3.)[11]

Within six months, they had then been forwarded on the *Queen Charlotte* brig to Rev. Marsden in Paramatta, New South Wales where Ellis noted he had seen them (Ellis 1969, II, 173). In October 1816, Marsden sent them on to the directors in London with an accompanying letter in which he explained that he now had "the unspeakable satisfaction of forwarding ... some of THE IDOL GODS OF OTAHEITE, as the glorious spoils of Idolatry; no event could have given me more pleasure" (Quarterly Chronicle of TMS, I, 161; Marsden to directors, 31 October 1816). These god images would form an early and important contribution to the Missionary Museum collection (see Wingfield, this volume), their status as trophies clearly defined. Marsden described them "now lying prostrate on the table before me" (*ibid*), each serving as an index of the heathen practice of islanders " ... and were we not certain of the fact, we could not believe that any human beings could place their salvation in these wretched images, and offer up human sacrifices to avert their anger" (*ibid*).

Once in London they were publicly announced in an engraving entitled 'The Family Idols of Pomare' (Figure 1) which appeared in the evangelical publication *Missionary Sketches III* (October 1818). Seven Tahitian idols or *to'o,* replete with feather and fibre attachments, appeared to hover rather sinisterly above two wooden figures or *ti'i* and these in turn flanked a still more unusual carving, identified as no. 9 – an upright baton with

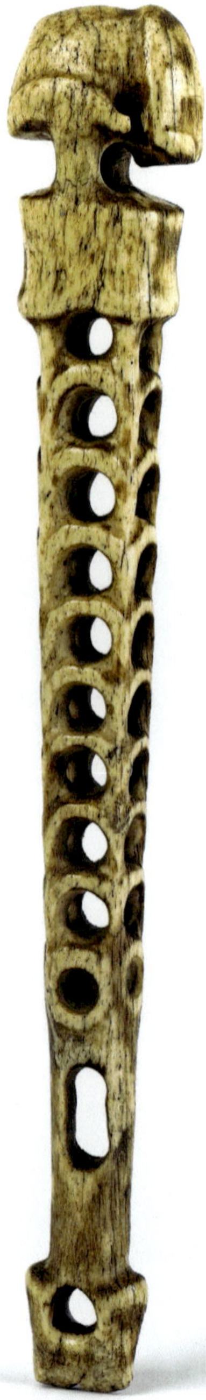

Figure 2. Whalebone tahiri. Oc, LMS 57 British Museum, London. Length 24.2cm.
Courtesy of the Trustees of the British Museum.

11 Missionary journals, reports, correspondence and official missionary publications including *Missionary Sketches* and *Quarterly Chronicle of Transactions of the Missionary Society* are housed in the Council for World Mission (CWM), Archives & Special Collections, School of Oriental and African Studies Library (SOAS), University of London).

Figure 3. Whale ivory and sinnet-bound tahiri. 1978.412.875, Metropolitan Museum of Art, New York. Length 27.9cm. Courtesy The Metropolitan Museum of Art, www.metmuseum.org.

rounded finial and base, a series of curiously arched canopies punched along its length. Descriptions in the accompanying legend reinforced their visual perplexity: alien and unknowable, missionaries alleged to have been rather disturbed by their strangeness – the accompanying text announced "they differ from anything we remember to have seen or read of, which has been used by idolaters for the purpose of worship" (*Missionary Sketches III*, October 1818, 2).

Item no. 9 can now be identified as LMS 57 (Figure 2), a *tahiri* or flywhisk handle currently in the Oceania collections of the British Museum following its transfer from the London Missionary Society (LMS) collections in 1890. Carved from a single section of whalebone, it is easily manipulated in the hand. Large perforations at its base would likely have incorporated fibre bindings extending below in a tail or whisk, but these are now lost. The engraved illustration gives little indication that the highly sculptural finial is in fact a figure, now heavily eroded – a clue to the fact that it has been handled extensively over time. Raised features indicate an oval face with two crescents for eyes and subtly discerned contours reveal a backward arching figure with thighs flexed to expose the vagina, in counterpoint to the phallic tip, referencing the glans of the penis, at its opposite end. This arched figure was likely a reference to birthing, or more specifically, transition across thresholds. Described in the missionary literature as flywhisks or fans, these *tahiri* were literally fanned or whisked in bold gestural movements to attract, or beckon, gods to presence from the dark reaches of *te po* during ritual practice in *te ao* – the world of the living.

Coveted for its rarity, this carved stem of whalebone is particularly potent. Whales in particular were deemed to be the *ata,* the shadow or embodiment of Ta'aroa, the original *atua* or god from whom all others derived. Their bones were not merely symbolic or ornamental, they were relics which quite literally contained the essence of Ta'aroa. Strong and lasting they were his *iho* or essence made permanent. Since the bones of one were also deemed to be the bones of all, this artefact worked metonymically to index the entire lineage and all its members. The serial canopies painstakingly hollowed out along its length were therefore intended as a highly abstracted, visual expression of fundamental genealogical principles.

Another flywhisk handle in the Metropolitan Museum of Art in New York (Figure 3) has a similarly distinctive, yet far more discernable, backward-arching figure. Balanced on a wide collar at one end, the figure infers a hollow space or canopy from which the central stem extends in a series of openwork sections bound into the whole. The carving on these varies from angular sections with minimal intervention to more complex sections incorporating highly stylised figures which support each corner, those with outstretched arms and legs giving way to a series of simple incisions which indicate facial features on highly abstracted figures. Most strikingly, the tip remains largely uncarved: the final series of carved detail fading into the smooth creamy surface of whale ivory.

Intriguingly all seven *tahiri* identified in museum collections around the world (Jessop [Nuku] 2007, 169-186) incorporate some indication of this arched component which specifically creates a canopy at the summit with a series of hollowed crescents extending below. In terms of Polynesian cosmology, the canopy inferred by this arched figure is a reference to a point of origin in terms of space and time, since the raising of the sphere of the sky was the moment which preceded the creation of man when Ta'aroa was said to have created the universe (Henry 1928, 161).

Propping up the sky

Islanders imagined the universe as a vast immensity which surrounded and enclosed them: missionary William Ellis (1969, III, 168) reported from his discussions with islanders that "they imagined that the sea which surrounded their islands was a level plane, and that at the visible horizon, or some distance beyond it, the sky, or *rai* [*ra'i*], joined the ocean, enclosing as with an arch, or hollow cone, the islands in the immediate vicinity". Cosmological accounts described the originator god Ta'aora as locked in the dark, empty void of *te po* – a realm associated with the night, ancestors and spirits. Pecking his way through the shell dome in which he was encased, Ta'aroa was said to have conjured forth gods in the night (referred to as *Atua fanau po*, that is "Gods born of, or brought forth from [the] Darkness or Eternal Night" (Morrison in Smith and Thomas 2013:196). Creating a world of light from the void of darkness, he had pushed against its limits, pecking his way through the shell which enveloped him to overturn the empty dome and raise it up to form the canopy of the sky. This canopy was then envisaged as further receding into a series of bounded spheres, each individually named, with the tenth layer unfolding finally into *te po*. This tenth sphere, the most remote in terms of time and distance from the earth, was considered to be the abode of the principal gods. Referred to as *te ra'i ha'amama no Tane,* it was conceived of as a gaping or 'yawning' opening which unfolded into perpetual darkness. Furthermore, the term *ha'amama* (meaning to open the mouth, to gape or yawn (Davies 1851 [1961], 89)) bears further connotations of birthing, so that each of these spheres or skies was envisaged as unfolding and opening out each into the next – ideas which were supported conceptually by the backward arching figure presiding over the top of each of these *tahiri*.

These prestigious ritual artefacts were known generically in Tahiti as *to'o*. Literally intended as posts or supports with which to prop up the sky, the term was particularly apt. For islanders they functioned as a means of engaging with *atua* or gods who dwelt on the other side of existence, a direct channel between two complementary realms – for if *te po* was associated with an extraordinary domain of darkness and night, then *te ao* was a world of light and life in which ordinary human endeavour took place. *Tahiri* might usefully be understood as a highly specific sub-category of *to'o* and their description as fans – from the verb *tahiri* (Davies 1851 [1961], 242) – is particularly compelling since we know that vigorous fanning encouraged the presence of *atua* (gods) who were said to bear down on the wind.

Luminosity and sound were other devices used to attract and summon the presence of gods and in particular Oro's arrival into *te ao* was said to be accompanied by the dynamic arching of a rainbow which stretched from the dome of the sky to earth amidst flashes of lightning and thunder. This is particularly instructive when we note the accompanying legend to 'The Family Idols of Pomare' (Figure 1) identifies LMS 57 as 'Tahi[r]i Anunaehau' – *anuanua* referring to a rainbow (*ibid*, 24) and *hau* – which as well as the more usual meaning of breath, wind and air can also serve as a qualifying adjective meaning to move beyond, in terms of something greater, larger and more significant (*ibid*, 99). In that sense, *Anu[a]n[u]ehau* would infer the greatest, most magisterial rainbow.

It is likely that the lustre and brightness inferred in the name, and indexed materially in the selection of whalebone and ivory for these fans aimed at establishing conditions appropriate for ritual. This as well as specifically referencing both the vertical and horizontal dimensions which connote the auspicious moment when light was first created from darkness, when Ta'aroa pushed up the dome of the sky to create light and space between two now separated spheres. Whilst Joseph Banks and other early visitors to Tahiti had encountered these kinds of objects in wood – referring to them rather bleakly as flywhisks or 'fly-flaps' – we can begin to see that in fact these were highly sophisticated and complex cosmological artefacts which supported the landscape both literally and conceptually.

In correspondence with missionaries

Specific references to the collection of objects by missionaries are rare in the archive. Yet significantly two of these ivory fans are specifically recorded as having been presented by Pomare II 'king' of Tahiti to the Rev. Dr. Thomas Haweis, a founding director of the Missionary Society in London and its former Chairman, in 1818. It was commonly assumed that Haweis was presented with each fan by Pomare II in person. However, whilst Haweis was certainly the Society's staunchest promoter back in metropolitan England, it transpires that he never set foot on Tahiti. In a letter written in Tahiti by Pomare II on 3rd October 1818 to the Rev. Haweis we now know that it was Pomare II himself who had led this particular initiative. Towards the end of the letter, the Tahitian chief explains that he now forwards "two little fans which the royal families of these countries, were accustomed to fan themselves with, when the day of the festival arrived & the king was prayed for"[12] and finishes with a note that all his family idols, except for a small one now also enclosed, are burned. This last he explains is Ta'aroa: "all of the large Idols are consumed, having been burned in the fire this is only a little one that remains" (*ibid*). In the same way that the extreme potency of god images required appropriate action in terms of managing *tapu* (a state of extreme sanctity or sacredness) in Polynesia, the *ari'i rahi* of Tahiti now saw the value of their insinuation into a highly expansive network of relations with significant chiefs identified in far-away England. In this they operated much as whalebone and ivory artefacts had always

12 CWM/South Seas Incoming Box 3A Jacket B Folder 7; Letter from Pomare to Haweis, dated Tahiti October 3 1818.

done: as material expressions of the reciprocal obligations between partners in exchange. The 'Family Idols of Pomare' operated as an effective means of binding Haweis and his associate Missionary Society directors to the genealogical network of the Pomare dynasty in Tahiti. Furthermore, this long-distance presentation of *tapu* artefacts was consistent with protocols of exchange throughout Polynesia: it created a debt and enhanced the status of the giver. The Tahitian chief and his missionary counterpart were now bound irrevocably to each other. Most strikingly, the circulation of potent artefacts – *things* at once intriguing and powerful – played a crucial role in this domain.

Female Statuette, Tonga

Andy Mills

This female statuette, currently housed at the Auckland Museum (AM32651), is believed to have been hung by the neck in 1830 as an act of iconoclasm – its hangman the influential Tongan chief Taufa'āhau, who had recently converted to Christianity. This hanging has taken on great significance in modern Tonga, one of the world's most devoutly Christian countries. The circumstances surrounding this key event in the history of Tongan Christianity merit closer examination, however, and illustrate that the missionised Tongans of the early 19th century were far from naive and passive recipients of the gospel. Indeed, it was rather the Protestant missionaries who naively entered a world of immense political complexity, becoming pawns as much as players in that world. The Reverend John Williams of the London Missionary Society (LMS) took this statuette back to England, and a label written in his own hand is gummed to her back, which reads:

Goddess of Lefuga hung by Taufaahau on embracing Christianity, Hapai, July, 1830.

In July 1830, Taufa'āhau was the thirty-three-year-old paramount chief of Ha'apai, an influential chiefdom of twenty-two islands in central Tonga, which he ruled from its capital Lifuka. Taufa'āhau was a formidable politician and warlord who dominated 19th-century Tonga, and this statuette's close link to his conversion renders it a key relic of Christian history in Western Polynesia. Over the twenty-five years following its hanging, Taufa'āhau reunified Tonga's several warring chiefdoms into a stable monarchy, as they had been in the 18th century. His Christianity was instrumental to this political reunion in three main ways: first, it attracted local military allies eager to support fellow Christians. Second, it provided a revolutionary cosmology which liberated chiefs and commoners alike from the many everyday inconveniences of the pagan *tapu* system, a complex set of beliefs obliging ritual observances to avoid sickness caused by contact with social superiors and supernatural beings. Third, Christian adherence attracted Western naval support and facilitated privileged access to imported steel tools and firearms. Weighed against such benefits, conversion also turned his non-Christian contemporaries against him, and embroiled him in a bloody religious war that ground on until 1852 (Campbell 2001, 72ff.). Because his conversion in July 1830

Figure 1. Female Statuette, AM32651. Image courtesy of Ethnology, Auckland War Memorial Museum - Tamaki Paenga Hira.

was to have such an impact on Tongan history, therefore, this statuette embodies an important political relationship between Taufa'āhau and his contemporaries, both Christian and non-Christian.

Equally, although this figure was collected by John Williams of the LMS, all missionary activity in Tonga at this time was directed by the Wesleyan Methodist Missionary Society (MMS). Consequently, the statuette also embodies a relationship between these two missionary organisations that requires elaboration here. The LMS was the first missionary organisation to introduce Christianity to Western Polynesia, landing ten male British missionaries on the largest Tongan island, Tongatapu, in 1797. By 1800, three had been killed in a local war, one had abandoned Christianity to marry a Tongan and the remainder had fled. Twenty-two years later, the Wesleyan Methodist Mission in Tonga began work on Tongatapu under the leadership of the Reverend Walter Lawry, and was fully established in 1826 by the Reverends John Thomas and John Hutchinson (Latukefu 1969). In its early years, the mission was heavily reliant on the economically-motivated hospitality of Ata, a powerful pagan ruler of Tongatapu's western district Hihifo. Without significant chiefly sanction, the Methodists gained converts very slowly, while Ata became increasingly frustrated by the impertinence and criticism of his foreign guests. This mission almost foundered too, but this was prevented by two key events in 1827. Firstly, the Reverends Nathaniel Turner and William Cross arrived from Britain to bolster the work. More importantly, however, the mission had a watershed success in converting the high-ranking chief Aleamotu'a.

Aleamotu'a was the paternal uncle of Tupouto'a, the most recent Tu'i Kanokupolu (working king) who had died in 1820 (Urbanowicz 1977). Aleamotu'a had been passed over in the royal succession in favour of Tupouto'a, but the latter's death rendered him heir to the throne once more. Despite this legitimate claim, the self-interested chiefs of Tongatapu refused to appoint Aleamotu'a in a bid to maintain control of the main island (Bott 1982). Aleamotu'a's conversion to Christianity in September 1827, however, raised the possibility that Christianity could become the state cult, and the chiefs decided to take preventative action. Reasoning that Aleamotu'a's desire to be king outweighed his attachment to the new faith, the non-Christian chiefs of Tongatapu offered to appoint him on the condition that he abandon the new religion. Strategically agreeing, Aleamotu'a was duly installed, but within months he publically resumed his Christian worship. As the number of Christian converts snowballed throughout central and eastern Tongatapu, Aleamotu'a's deception came to be bitterly resented by Ata and the people of Hihifo; western Tongatapu became so hostile to Christianity that it became necessary to abandon the mission there early in 1829 in order to minimise bloodshed.

As the unrest on Tongatapu grew, Aleamotu'a hastily pressurised his network of loyal chiefs throughout the archipelago to convert. Foremost among this cohort was Taufa'āhau, his great-nephew, the son of Tupouto'a, and heir to the working kingship. So it was that (despite no prior interest in Christianity) Taufa'āhau responded to Aleamotu'a's wishes later that year and requested that the Reverend John Thomas establish a mission in Ha'apai. Although worshipping the patron deity of one's superiors was common practice in Tonga, Taufaʻāhau's initial motivations were largely economic and political: the Wesleyans distributed imports, hosted most Western visitors, and acted as their mediators and translators with the locals. Evidently doubtful of Taufaʻāhau's intentions, Thomas declined to go himself but sent Pita Vi, one of the first Tongans to be baptised, with a stipulation that Taufaʻāhau must renounce his pagan idolatry to Vi's satisfaction, before a Western missionary would be sent. This is an important point: Taufaʻāhau hanging this statuette was no spontaneous act of iconoclasm; the Methodists had explicitly requested the abandonment of "idols" as a precondition to his fulfilling his duty to Aleamotuʻa. After experimentally testing the wrath of several powerful deities, and finding them unable or unwilling to punish him, Taufaʻāhau quickly set about satisfying Thomas's demands; deconsecrating temples to accommodate his concubines, and gathering together a collection of the deity vessels and other supernaturally empowered objects (*fakafaʻanga*) that were deposited within them (Van der Grijp 2002, 255). By January 1830, Thomas and his wife had moved to Lifuka to fulfil their side of the bargain and establish a mission house (Latukefu 1969, 98-100). On 12 February, Thomas (quoted in Larsson 1960, 59n70) reported how Taufaʻāhau presented him with four statuettes of this kind as an explicit symbol of his renunciation of idolatry:

> *It will gladden the hearts of friends of Mission to learn that these idols which were once adored as gods are now cast away as a useless thing. The Houses which were once dedicated to these idols are now inhabited by those that worshipped them, and they are now sanctified by the word of the living God and by prayer.*

Four months later, on 11 June, Thomas called at Taufaʻāhau's home, and there observed five more statuettes, hung from the roof beams with cords around their necks. Around the same date, Taufaʻāhau also sent statuettes to Thomas's colleagues Nathaniel Turner and William Cross on Tongatapu, indicating the strategic reuse of these statuettes as diplomatic gifts to cement his relationship with the mission. Hooper (2006, 242) rightly questions whether this hanging was truly the desecration that Thomas interpreted it to be; strangulation was the standard method of performing and consecrating a human sacrifice throughout Western Polynesia. Moreover, contemporary descriptions of both sacred weapons in Tonga, and the closely cognate ivory statuettes of neighbouring Fiji, indicate that such spirit-containing artefacts were normally suspended on cords inside god houses when supernaturally activated (Clunie 1986, 109-10; David *et al.* 2004, 135). It is therefore extremely unlikely that suspension represented a sincere act of iconoclasm for Taufaʻāhau, although he clearly felt it necessary to impress that idea upon Thomas. Something often overlooked in discussions of these statuettes is that they were seized punitively from the tombs and temples of Taufaʻāhau's insubordinate petty chiefs, and were therefore uninvolved with his own ancestral cult; if he was giving up "idols", they were not his own. Furthermore, five years later in 1835, Taufaʻāhau erected an enlarged Methodist chapel at Lifuka in which he reused sacred clubs and spears (believed to contain spirits and possess *mana* or supernatural efficacy) in the construction of its Communion rails and pulpit newels (Tucker 1836, 319). Like the statuette hangings, the Methodist missionaries read such acts as "swords beaten into ploughshares" (Isaiah 2:4), but Taufa'āhau's Tongan contemporaries would have clearly understood them to be empowering incorporations of pre-existing spirit-objects into the fabric of his home and his patron deity's temple respectively.

Towards the end of June 1830, John Williams and Charles Barff of the LMS arrived at Tongatapu *en route* to establish a mission in Samoa. They held a historic meeting with Nathaniel Turner, where they agreed that the MMS should concentrate its efforts in Tonga and Fiji, while the LMS should oversee the Protestant mission in Samoa. As well as ensuring that Tonga would become an overwhelmingly Wesleyan nation, this was a vital act of ecumenical politics, eliminating competition and the reduplication of labour between different protestant British missions in Western Polynesia. Underlying it, however, was the need to settle an awkward fact: the intrusion of the MMS upon a missionary field first opened, unsuccessfully, by the LMS thirty years earlier. This cooperative spirit followed Williams and Barff to Lifuka on 8 July, where Thomas welcomed them warmly, and presented Williams with one of the four statuettes he had received that February. Williams and Barff then had a brief audience with Taufa'āhau, who presented Williams with the Auckland Museum statuette. Williams (1837, 318-20) recorded Taufa'āhau's words at this time:

Figure 2. The hanging of the statuette, as Williams represented it eleven years later. (Williams 1843, 274).

"They are worthless, they are pieces of wood, they are devils; but we were formerly in the dark: It is only lately that our hearts have been made light in the knowledge of the true God". On observing five goddesses hanging by the neck, I requested this intrepid chief to give me one of them, which he immediately cut down and presented to me.

Besides the stylistic resonance of these words with the rhetoric of most Protestant missionary writings of the time, Neich (2007, 237) observes that Williams' three accounts of this event disagree about several basic details, and consequently their accuracy is doubtful. What is clear, however, is this particular figure's significance to Williams as an emblem of Protestant Christianity taking unshakeable root in Tonga irrespective of which missionary organisation achieved it:

I prize it the more highly, because it was one of the trophies of the moral conquest of the Gospel, achieved by Christians of another denomination. It shows us, that God does not intend to convert the world by any one section of his church. (Williams 1841, 275)[13]

Williams mentions an incidental fact about his brief visit to Lifuka which goes some way towards placing these diplomatic "idol" presentations in a more fleshed-out local context: when Williams and Barff landed, Taufa'āhau was occupied with playing host to a major diplomatic delegation led by his powerful northern neighbour Finau 'Ulukalala III, the ruler of Vava'u. Barely a handful of chiefs had comparable political and military power to Taufa'āhau, but 'Ulukalala was the strongest of them. He had conspired against Taufa'āhau in war only four years earlier, and moreover, was bitterly opposed to the spread of Christianity, having wholly prohibited the founding of a mission at Vava'u.[14] Fearing that Taufa'āhau would follow Aleamotu'a in converting, 'Ulukalala's diplomatic mission to Ha'apai had the specific aim of dissuading him. During this visit, 'Ulukalala made Taufa'āhau a generous gift of a large new warship and indulged in various martial games; we can suspect a threatening subtext behind these acts, because Taufa'āhau had the ship hauled out of the water and chopped up for firewood.

Seen in this context, Taufa'āhau's alliance with the missionaries embodied by this statuette becomes a direct act of political defiance towards 'Ulukalala. What was actually at stake during 'Ulukalala's diplomatic mission to Ha'apai was not Taufa'āhau's support for Christianity's doctrines, however, but rather his support for Aleamotu'a as the legitimate successor to the working kingship. Taufa'āhau's thinly veiled but very public rejection of 'Ulukalala's intervention tells a compelling story. Rather than a moment of religious conversion, this statuette's presentation marks the moment at which Taufa'āhau obliged 'Ulukalala to decide whether he would drive Vava'u into alliance with the pagan enemies of the legitimate working king Aleamotu'a (and Taufa'āhau's Ha'apai), or accept a Christianised, Westernised future for the archipelago. Undoubtedly a hard decision for him, 'Ulukalala's

---

13 Sadly, it seems unlikely that a Catholic mission would have evoked the same fraternal sentiments.

14 J. E. Moulton [n.d.]. *Notes on Tongan History and Tongan Legends by the Reverend J. E. Moulton.* Pacific Manuscripts Bureau Microfilm No. 3, 17-20.

choice is made clear by the fact that his position changed completely thereafter: he himself converted to Methodism the following year, burning his temples and their contents over three spectacular nights. With his alliance, Taufa'āhau controlled the northern half of Tonga, and would wage open war on the pagans of Hihifo within five years (Campbell 2001, 72ff.).

The hanging and gifting of these Tongan statuettes in July 1830 are unlikely to have marked Taufa'āhau's conversion. The Reverend David Cargill (1841, 44, 76) recorded that Taufa'āhau was expelled from the Methodist congregation in 1831 for "sin", and only permitted to be baptised later that year when he had relinquished polygamy. Cargill himself believed that Taufa'āhau's first genuine experience of Christian faith occurred four years later, on 31 July 1834, when he collapsed and experienced an ecstatic state during the mass conversion events that swept through northern Tonga at that time. Before this time, however, we should take a less polarised view of the relationship between his traditional practices and Christianity; like many of his contemporaries, his Christian practice throughout the 1830s was heavily blended with the religious practices of his youth. Beyond this, it seems clear that his renowned strategic cunning (which would ultimately secure him the throne) enabled him to devise forked actions that were effective both locally and internationally, in radically different ways. His presentation of these statuettes is a prime example of this strategy, which allowed him to steer a narrow course through the reefs of political and ideological conflict that beset Tonga at the time.

For John Williams, John Thomas and the other Protestant missionaries, it is evident that a cosmology informed by the Old Testament struggles of Israel with its heathen neighbours, the second Commandment (Exodus 20: 4-6), and opposition to Catholic sacred imagery, profoundly motivated them to seek out and capture the anthropomorphic "idols" of major deities in Tonga, as they did elsewhere in Polynesia. Although such statuettes are very unlikely to have been major Tongan deities or images of them, their conformity to an established "idol" concept made them valuable commodities in a complex emerging economy of faith, power and politics.

EXHIBITION AND SALE AT THE WESLEYAN CENTENARY HALL, BISHOPSGATE-STREET WITHIN; FOR THE WESLEYAN MISSIONARY SOCIETY.—(SEE NEXT PAGE.)

Illustration of an Exhibition and Sale at the Wesleyan Centenary Hall, United Kingdom

Steven Hooper

An illustration of an "Exhibition and Sale" (Figure 1) which took place on 12-13 June 1851 at the Wesleyan Centenary Hall in London, conveniently coinciding with the Great Exhibition that brought huge numbers of people to the capital, was published in the *Illustrated London News* of 21 June 1851 (page 579). It shows large Fijian and Tongan barkcloths hanging from posts, draped in front of paintings and suspended from a line. Two bowls, one a four-legged kava/*yaqona* bowl filled with short clubs, can be seen in the centre of the floor, flanked by two racks of larger clubs and paddles. Spears can be seen arrayed at the back of the room and elsewhere. A distinctive long narrow Fijian bark cloth with offset block designs hangs down the inside of the opening on the right hand side. On the left a couple admire a sheet of bark cloth at a stall, the front of which is hung with two distinctive Fiji-style rectangular baskets. The grand room projects an atmosphere of civilised gentility as the elegantly dressed ladies and gentlemen pore over the "offerings" of people from far-off lands. The accompanying text lists the range of items on display, including some not visible in the illustration, such as "a 'Mburi' or *Feejee Temple*" and "an immense rope contributed by the King at the missionary meeting at Lakemba". "Idols", also not illustrated, are described as "rather symbols than images, such as elephants' and whales' teeth, which represent, indeed, the chief divinity".

The offering up of "idols" to missionaries by newly converted islanders had occurred in Tonga and elsewhere in Polynesia at an earlier date (see Mills, this volume, and Hooper 2007; 2008). Besides advocating the destruction of pagan idols, however, missionaries encouraged their preservation, motivated by a desire for trophies to be displayed in missionary museums as evidence of evangelical success. These trophy displays performed an additional function, as mechanisms for fund-raising, whereby the visiting public, moved by missionary labours and the desirability of salvation for benighted heathens, made donations to assist the missionary effort. Missionaries in the field suffered chronic funding problems and

Figure 1. Exhibition and Sale at the Wesleyan Centenary Hall, 12-13 June 1851. *The Illustrated London News*, 21 June 1851, page 579.

in Fiji a local response to these budgetary difficulties was to encourage a type of gift-giving festival (*soli*), which derived from indigenous pre-Christian inter-clan or inter-chiefdom exchanges (*sōlevu*, literally "large gatherings"). *Soli* and *basā* (bazaars) continue to this day in Fiji as fund-raising mechanisms for churches, schools, sports clubs and other causes. In Tonga the missionaries also benefitted from offerings called *me'a'ofa* (gifts; literally "love things"), which during a visit in 1847 by Reverend Walter Lawry included clubs, spears, mats, combs, baskets and wooden pillows (Lawry 1850, 13, 19, 21). Lawry appeared comfortable with the pagan origins of *me'a'ofa*, reflecting: "At my first visit [1822-3] I saw these offerings brought and laid at the shrine of the false gods, and connected with much that was immoral and cruel. They have now changed their object of worship, and their mode of conducting this ancient practice. The Missionaries have done wisely to control, but not to destroy, the thank-offerings of the people" (Lawry 1850, 13).

This paper will outline two mechanisms by which missionaries acquired local offerings and turned them into commodities to help finance their activities – the *soli* and the bazaar (*basā*).

Methodist missionaries in Fiji in the 19th century were not only concerned for the souls of Fijians; they were anxious about money and about the education of their children. As Henderson explains (Williams 1931, 407-8), sending them to England to live with guardians was hard to contemplate, and setting up a school in Fiji, scattered and precarious as the missions were in the 1840s, proved difficult. The welcome solution proposed in 1847 by Reverend Walter Lawry was to establish a school in Auckland for the children of missionaries based in New Zealand, Tonga and Fiji. The Methodist mission ship, *John Wesley*, would provide transport to and from the islands and the school would safeguard the children from unsuitable (if probably enjoyable) Fijian influences. Of their anxieties in this regard, Lawry wrote, "our utmost efforts to prevent them from being injured by the example and spirit of the natives are unavailing" (Lawry 1850, 45-6), while James Calvert (1858, 219) reported that alarming instances "had even occurred in which the children of Missionaries had learned to speak in the language of the people, while an acquaintance with that of their parents was never gained". The new school in Auckland was partly to be financed by the missionaries themselves, but, given their relative penury, they needed to raise funds from local sources, so the existing bazaar method was chosen. Lawry, as General Superintendent of Wesleyan Missions in the region, was in 1847 on an inspection tour of missions in Tonga and Fiji in the *John Wesley*, and at the same time was collecting produce to sell at a bazaar to finance the building of a chapel in Auckland. The new school was to be financed in the same way, which mainly involved encouraging offerings from converted islanders, as the following examples show.

At the district meeting at Viwa, Fiji, in late September, 1847, Lawry recorded that "contributions have been made in the Vewa [Viwa] Circuit, consisting of mats, native cloth, pigs, yams, &c., amounting in value here to £16.2.10d". On 5 October, he wrote, "The School-Examination took place at Vewa. The procession was composed of almost the entire population. The Chief, with a grey beard, walked before; each person, whether old or young, bore a thank-offering – a mat, a club, or an earthenware vessel of native manufacture, &c. These, by the kindness of the Missionaries here, as everywhere, were handed over to me for the Auckland Chapel Bazaar" (Lawry 1850, 45, 63). On 18 October Lawry recorded another method of obtaining artefacts for sale. "An elderly woman has just called here to exchange her native dress, about eight inches wide, made to wrap round the middle. For this she wished to obtain some calico to cover her person; as she began to *lotu* [convert to Christianity] yesterday ... Of course, we gave her the calico; and I shall take her *lego* [*liku*, fibre skirt], or garment, to the bazaar at Auckland, to assist us, by its sale, in building the house of the Lord" (Lawry 1850, 70). On arriving with Thomas Williams a few days later at the new mission station at Bua, Lawry noted that mats and coconut oil were given to Williams, and that "many fine pieces of sandal-wood were handed to me. These must go to the Auckland chapel bazaar". Continuing to Nadi, also on Vanua Levu, on 10 November there was another presentation by local converts: "Every one had his present in his hand; consisting of either a large mat, or a club, a spear, a shell, a *lego*, (female dress), fowls, cocoa-nut oil, or some food ready dressed" (Lawry 1850, 83, 87).

This pattern of thank-offering collection, which also resembled the periodic *lala* "tribute" collecting undertaken by Fijian chiefs, continued for some years. On 18 October 1848, at Bua, Williams recounts (1931, 452): 'Held our school feast. It was amusing to see the people bringing their offerings in return for the expected distribution of books – sails, mats, *masis* [bark cloths], [coco]nuts, clubs, spears, bottles of oil, trumpet shells, baskets, ti-root [*Cordyline*], sandalwood, fishing nets, fishing hook (Tongan), fans, oil dish, yangona [*sic*] root and two native beaters [for bark cloth]. Such a medley collection I had never seen before". By this stage "books", printed New Testaments and sermons, viewed as power objects that connected converts to the Christian god, were clearly in demand, and were considered by Fijians to be appropriate exchange items for a range of local produce. It is not clear whether the missionaries interpreted the inclusion of clubs and spears as symbolic of the rejection of warfare, but such presentations had their origins in pre-Christian *madrali* offerings, about which Williams noted (1858, 231): "Clubs, spears, and other valuable articles are thus consecrated to the gods. I am told that many men, after killing an enemy, offer a spear to the priest, in order to insure protection from the spears of the enemy on future occasions". Williams is very likely to have been aware of the sacrificial nature of these "offerings"; he had arrived in Fiji in 1840 and was familiar with *sōlevu* exchanges that included valuables such as mats, barkcloth, clubs, spears, bowls and scented coconut oil.

Sōlevu-type exchanges of artefacts for books (and blessings) became a well-established practice, apparently driven as much by local religious/cultural energy as by missionary need for commodities to sell to finance their school. On 3 May 1849 Williams records at Bua that the people "had a kind of *solevu* at their own desire. They presented 115 yams, 20 spears, as many clubs, a sunshade [large fan] and seven mats. In return they received 200 or more books and fly sheets. They were over-zealous to get the books into their possession, and made much noise" (Williams 1931, 485). These exchanges appear to have suited both parties, engaged as they were in different forms of wealth and abundance creation.

The school for missionary children opened in Auckland in November 1849 and collecting for bazaars continued. The 1850 voyage round the islands resulted in substantial contributions towards the anticipated costs of refitting the *John Wesley*. In August, at Tubou, Lakeba, Lau, Thomas Williams reported (1931, 526): "The people assembled in the afternoon to present their gifts, and so liberal were they that it is thought the spears, clubs, cloth, &c. contributed will sell for £100 or more. Scarcely were we out of chapel when the *Wesley* was shouted [shouts of sail-ho]... After a push we got a large quantity of bowls, boxes &c. on board". The scale of contributions probably reflected that fact that the local paramount chief, Tui Nayau, had converted to Christianity in 1849, encouraging many of his people to divert their offerings to the Wesleyan priests. The bowls are likely to have been four-legged *tanoa*-type bowls for kava (*yaqona*), made in southern Lau and brought to Lakeba for presentation, a practice which still occurs for Methodist meetings and chiefly gatherings.

The *John Wesley* delivered Williams back to Bua, where on 10 September 1850 there was another offering (Williams 1931, 529-31):

> *... they came in three companies chanting merrily, each man, woman and child carrying conspicuously his or her 'subscription'... We counted – pieces of –*

Sandalwood, 180	*Clubs, 11*	*Tumeric [sic], 1 cake*
Mosquito curtains [barkcloth], 12	*Hand [throwing] clubs, 27*	*Masi [barkcloth], 1*
Bau mats, 3	*Sunshades, 3*	*Tongan fish hook*
Kulas [decorated] and sail mats, 2	*Neck ornaments, 6*	*Tongan pillow*
Sinnet [coir cord], small rolls, 2	*Likus [fibre dresses], 24*	*Tongan basket of shells*
Walking-sticks [staffs], 14	*Mat dresses, 2*	*Tongan fish line*
Fancy baskets, 3	*A flesh fork*	*Spears, 38*

James Calvert later explained the intended purpose of these offerings (1858, 216):

> *After the "Wesley" had successfully completed her third voyage among the islands in 1850, it was found necessary that she should return to England for repairs, and to have tanks fitted in her for the cocoa-nut oil which was collected at the different Stations... To help to defray the expense of the homeward voyage, the native Christians were requested to contribute specimens of their manufactures, productions, and curiosities. To this they readily agreed, and the "Wesley" left the islands with considerable native stores, and sailed for England... The native contributions which she brought were tastefully displayed at the Centenary Hall, and the sale of them superintended by ladies, who kindly undertook the task. More than a thousand visitors inspected this novel bazaar, and upwards of four hundred pounds was the pecuniary result.*

But what became of all these clubs, spears, barkcloths and other items that had been offered to the missionaries at *soli* and *me'a'ofa* in return for books, sermons and the approbation of the Christian god, and had then been sold off by the missionaries at bazaars in Auckland, London (and probably Sydney)? Some items may have been retained for the Methodist Missionary Museum in London, but it seems that the majority was sold into private ownership without documentation. Many of these objects will have eventually found their way into museum collections in Britain, New Zealand and Australia, but their particular collection histories are mostly lost.

And what of those remote peoples, and the methods by which these objects left their lands? As we have seen, Lawry was well aware of the importance of encouraging continuity of sacrificial ritual practice in the new Christian context – he even approved of the re-use of a pagan temple at Viwa as a chapel (1850, 39). From a local perspective, the route to abundance and prosperity was through the establishment of effective relationships with divine powers, manifested in sacrificial exchanges whereby offerings were made in return for blessings and divine favour. The power objects of the Christian priest/chiefs, notably books, as well as their medical expertise, which demonstrably prolonged life, were eagerly sought after, and local valuables such as clubs, spears, mats and bark cloth were willingly deployed as reciprocal offerings by appreciative recipients. After all, these things could easily be made again, whereas printing presses, industrial looms and medical equipment were at that time foreign and mysterious technologies not easy of access. In the case of the *soli* and *me'a'ofa* presentations, "cultural property" achieved its true value for the original makers through distribution and alienation, not retention. At the same time such things, previously retained by missionaries for fund-raising displays, were transformed into commodities and sold at bazaars such as the "Exhibition and Sale" in London in June 1851.

"Livingstone's Loom", Malawi

Sarah Worden

The Livingstone collection held at National Museums Scotland (NMS) is a small eclectic assemblage from central southern Africa. The objects include a stone mill for grinding corn, the jaw of a hippopotamus, rocks and minerals including coal and gold, as well as a hunters net woven from local baobab fibre. This diversity, one could argue, reveals no clear strategy for collecting based on either typology or category. Nevertheless, research into any one of these objects reveals insights into Dr David Livingstone's (1813–1873) engagements with the people he met, as well as his interests, which extended from ethnography to geology and natural sciences. This hand weaving loom (Figure 1), collected by Livingstone in Malawi, links his upbringing in Scotland to his subsequent life in Africa, as well as his particular vision for the continent's future, involving the three 'Cs': Christianity, Commerce and Civilisation. It also resonates strongly with the revival of traditions of craft production in Malawi today.

Livingstone, most often described as a missionary explorer, travelled throughout south and central Africa between 1841 and 1873, driven by a vision that Christianity and legitimate commerce could improve the quality of life for Africans and end the slave trade in central Africa. Livingstone made three journeys through Malawi, and many Malawians today regard Livingstone with great respect and affection for his efforts to end the slave trade there. Concerned by the need for Africa to cultivate products that Europe wanted to buy, in order that legitimate European commerce could penetrate Africa, Livingstone saw the potential for an economy based on cotton to displace the trade in slaves via east African ports. As he observed on his travels in southern Malawi:

> *The Lake people grow abundance of cotton for their own consumption, and can sell it for a penny a pound, or even less. Water-carriage exists by the Shire and Zambesi all the way to England...and it seems feasible that a legitimate and thriving trade might, in short time, take the place of the present unlawful traffic.* (Livingstone and Livingstone 2005, 114)

This potential was supported by John Kirk, botanist to the Livingstone Zambesi Expedition (1858–1864), who, reporting to the Royal Geographical Society, described in great detail the cultivation and use of native cotton in the region

Figure 1. The Livingstone collection fixed single-heddle ground loom (NMS A.762.2). Courtesy of National Museums Scotland.

where the loom was collected. He concluded that cotton seemed to be the crop best suited for these parts, and the people "an industrious race, already extensively engaged in the growth of cotton" (Kirk 1861-2, 27). Similarly, Livingstone observed that the expedition "scarcely entered a village in the upper and lower Shire Valleys without finding a number of men cleaning, spinning and weaving". As the expedition proceeded further north up the Shire River, Kirk reported that every village had large plantations of cotton of superior quality which "the natives grow for the manufacture of cloths", and Livingstone described the indigenous cotton, *tonje cadja*, as feeling like wool in the hand and producing a stronger cloth than from the *tonje manga*, non-native cotton which had been introduced into the region (although he does not specify its origin) (*ibid.*, 27; Livingstone and Livingstone 2005, 102).

The status of cloth production at that time is evident from Kirk's observation that "all engage in it from the chief to the poor people" (Kirk 1861-2, 28). It seems the region was largely self-sufficient in production and use, as Kirk notes that "they have never had the opportunity of selling cotton, but would readily enter into its growth on a large scale if they knew that it would be purchased in exchange for cloth and beads" (*ibid.*, 28). Here Kirk is referring to the much-desired imported European cloth which was common trading currency between Europeans and local chiefs elsewhere.

Perhaps Livingstone acquired the loom in exchange for such cloth? Livingstone travelled with large quantities of imported cloth, noting its exchange value for local goods, hospitality and services (Livingstone and Livingstone 2005, 45, 156). However, for all the recorded detail regarding cotton cultivation and weaving techniques from the expedition, including commissioning an engraving in *Narrative of an Expedition*, there is no mention of the acquisition of the loom (*ibid.*, 102).

The loom is an object which initially reveals little of its potential. It has the appearance of a bundle of sticks of roughly equal size entwined with lengths of cotton threads. But in the hands of a skilled weaver it was once a means for the expression of creativity and the production of income. It is an example of the type of fixed single-heddle ground loom used throughout south-eastern and central southern Africa. The design is such that both narrow and wide cloth could be produced, with minor adjustments to the frame and warp beams which are stretched out and fixed to the ground, (Davison & Harries 1980). Weaving was labour-intensive, as Livingstone observes, "all the processes being painfully slow" (Livingstone and Livingstone 2005, 103). However, the loom was practical in that it could be dismantled and rolled up with the length of cloth "in situ" when not in use and repositioned when time allowed for the weaver to return to the task. The loom was acquired by Livingstone with a piece of cloth in production: a coarse, durable cotton fabric, strong enough to be used for a hammock or awning. This loom was part of one of at least three separately recorded acquisitions from Livingstone. The Museum's Annual Reports produced in 1862 document receipt of the loom with other objects: "From Dr Livingstone also, we have received some curious illustrations of the manufactures of the natives of the banks of the

Zambesi and other districts of Africa"[15]... "African hand mill for grinding corn; loom and web from the Manganja [*sic*] country; iron bracelet from Mpemba, Manganja country; specimen of Manganja copper wire. Presented by the Rev. Dr Livingstone".[16] The Mang'anja people were settled across northern Mozambique and southern Malawi, and were well established in the Shire valley region where Livingstone had documented the extent of cotton production and use.

It has been suggested that Livingstone was not particularly drawn to material culture and was not a collector by nature (Cannizzo 1996, 141). However, the collection that Livingstone sent to the Museum suggests that he was aware of the aim of George Wilson, the Museum's first Director until his death in 1859, to collect technologies from non-industrial nations. Wilson had noted in his Annual Report for 1856 that "a correspondence accordingly has been opened with agents in different quarters of the globe..." where "intelligent men interested in the Museum have engaged to send examples of native manufactures of those countries" (1858, 161). Livingstone was one of these men, and also had a personal connection with Wilson. They had first met in 1838, in the chemistry laboratory of Thomas Graham at University College London, whilst he was a student and Wilson a demonstrator. The objects Livingstone sent to the museum were evidence of local resources, technologies and the potential for commercial enterprise, as outlined earlier, one of the key motivations for his exploration.

Livingstone would also have had a particular and personal interest in the production of cotton and African weaving technology, coming as he did from a background dominated by the cotton weaving industry on the banks of the River Clyde. From the age of ten until he joined the London Missionary Society in 1838, he worked in Blantyre Mill, first as a "piecer", tying together the broken threads between the spinning jennies, and later as a cotton spinner. It was here that Livingstone developed physically, spiritually and intellectually into the man who would spend over thirty years of his life in Africa (Mullen 2012, 15-31).

Whilst investigation into the history of the loom revealed these fascinating connections with Livingstone, a further unexpected link between the loom and contemporary weaving practice in Southern Malawi was recently uncovered. Although the Shire River region continues to be known as the cotton-growing centre of Malawi, many of the traditional uses of local cloth for currency and tribute, together with local clothing customs, changed dramatically with European colonisation. By the mid-1930s, the weaving skills in this region, which Livingstone had been so enthusiastic about fostering and developing, had largely died out. Concerns over this decline led to a heritage project, initiated by Museums of Malawi with the Mlambe Foundation in the Netherlands, which sought to change the situation, drawing on the knowledge and skills of the last remaining hand weaver in the area. At the newly built Tisunge! Heritage Centre in the Shire River Valley, cotton weaving skills were reintroduced to the region. It was a project which

---

15 Archer, T. C. 1862 [Report for the year 1861 on] Industrial Museum of Scotland. *In* Ninth Report of Science and Art Department, Appendix Y. *Parliamentary Papers (House of Commons Sessional Papers)* XXI [3022.], pp. 175-183 [519-527].

16 ibid; p.182.

Figure 2. Weavers Hendrix Lossan and Kennedy Mdalika at Tisunge! Heritage Centre, Chikwawa, Malawi, April 2012. Courtesy of National Museums Scotland.

aimed to ensure that traditional technologies were not completely lost, and was designed to promote tourism and generate local income. During NMS fieldwork in southern Malawi, samples of contemporary cotton weaving and spinning and weaving equipment were acquired for NMS collections, whilst observation of the weaving process led to further understanding of the technological aspects of the Livingstone loom. It is interesting that this recent revival again identified cotton hand weaving with commercial interest, resonating with Livingstone's earlier observations in the region. However, despite the aspirations for the centre as a tourist destination, it is currently closed due to lack of funding.

Like many museums with ethnographic collections, objects associated with missionaries entered the museum in Edinburgh during the late 19th and early 20th century in large numbers, collected within a framework shaped by the dissemination of Christianity and the expansion of the colonial enterprise. Prominent amongst these missionaries was David Livingstone, and the subsequent Scottish missionary engagement with Africa was in large part inspired by him. This loom collected by Livingstone, in many ways an unprepossessing object, nevertheless has the capacity to weave together past and present, to connect people and places, and to add to an understanding of African technologies and cultural practices. The dynamic potential of such missionary collected objects is revealed here through the resonances this object evokes between historic events that formed part of the missionary encounter, and contemporary efforts to develop and preserve threatened cultural practices.

125012.

Institution.
National Museum.
125012.

Bird Specimen, Papua New Guinea

Joshua A. Bell

In an acid-free cardboard box in a wooden drawer in the Bird Division of the Smithsonian Institution's National Museum of Natural History lies specimen 125012. Collected 135 years ago, specimen 125012 is identified as a moustached treeswift (*Hemiprocne mystacea*). The small bird is predominantly black and grey with bluish wings and distinct white banding on its head, from which its name derives. This bird's living kin inhabit the tropical lowland and montane forests and mangroves of the Indonesian archipelago, New Guinea and the Solomon Islands and they subsist on insects. As with other bird specimens, specimen 125012 was gutted soon after being caught to preserve its skin and feathers. Though not discernible, the bird was most likely shot. Its cavity is filled with cotton and has been sown shut with thread. Wrapped around the bird's body is a yellowed piece of paper held with a pin. The paper is inscribed with the specimen number, the bird's alternative scientific name (*Dendrochelidon mystacea*), and the following: "Port Moresby, New Guinea. Rev. W. G. Lawes". Tied to the bird's leg is an official museum tag, which repeats the same information, but has the name "H. B. Tristram" written instead. The two labels and the different names point to the ways in which many natural history specimens and cultural objects moved between people before coming to be part of particular collections. Specimen 125012 helps to illuminate some aspects of these networks, and the ways missionaries engaged one another and museums through various natural and cultural things.

Specimen 125012 is one of fifty-three birds that the Reverend Henry Baker Tristram gave to the then National Museum (now the National Museum of Natural History) as an exchange (Accession 23507; January 2, 1892). An avid collector of birds, and renowned for his writings on the Middle East, the English-born Rev. Tristram (1822–1906) sat at the centre of a network of scientific, missionary and amateur collectors. As he noted in the preface of his published catalogue (Tristam 1889, iii-iv),

> *For the last 20 years I have more particularly directed my attention to the fauna of Oceanic Islands—above all, those of the Pacific and Indian Oceans. In this research I have derived much assistance from the kindness of Naval Officers, Missionaries and Consuls…*

Figure 1. Two views of specimen 125012, a Moustached Treeswift (*Hemiprocne mystacea*) collected by the Rev. W. G. Lawes in Port Moresby, Papua New Guinea and donated to the Smithsonian Institution's National Museum by the Rev. H. B. Tristram in 1892. Photographs by author, 2014.

Tristram used his position as a founding member of the British Ornithologists' Union, as well as one of the governors of the Church Missionary Society, to establish this network with which he built up and dispersed an incredible array of birds. When he sold his collection in 1896 to the Liverpool Museum, it comprised 17,000 specimens of 6,000 species. By the time of his death, ten years later, he had amassed another 7,000 specimens of 3,000 species (Mearns & Mearns 1998, 242).

Accession 23507 is one of three exchanges Tristram had with the National Museum from 1879 to 1892. Such exchanges were another means by which he built up his collection (Tristram 1889). The accession to which specimen 125012 belongs is emblematic of the networks that Tristram relied on, and is composed of birds obtained by seven naturalist collectors including Tristram himself: Heinrich Bernstein (1828–1865), Henry O. Forbes (1852–1931), Andrew Goldie (1840–1891), Edgar L. Layard (1824–1900), Rev. W. G. Lawes (1839–1907), O. Linden (dates unknown), and Lieutenant G. E. Richards (dates unknown). Collected from 1863 to 1881, the birds came from nine localities: Duke of York Island; Durham, England; New Britain; New Caledonia; New Guinea; Solomon Islands; Sumatra; Ternate; and Vanuatu. While silent on how he obtained specimen 125012, Tristram obtained many of his specimens by mail from his correspondents. Revealing the, at times, tenuous nature of the means of procurement, he notes how in the case of "a small consignment of birds and eggs" sent by the Reverend J. Inglis from Vanuatu, "the box was about a year on its way to me, and the greater part of the contents, especially the parcel from Erromanga, have been utterly destroyed by damp and sea-water – so much so that many of the specimens are reduced to a mass of pulp, and utterly unrecognizable" (Tristram 1876, 260).

If this accession is revealing of collecting networks, it also points to the scientific work of missionaries (Sivasundaram 2005). Indeed, as long-term residents, missionaries were in a unique position to provide information to travelling explorers and scientists, as well as to collect for themselves. Natural history specimens were not only an important contribution to the types of knowledge missionaries helped document worldwide, but, alongside ethnographic materials, formed a significant but too often overlooked portion of what they collected and helped distribute (Gunson 1994). If Tristram as a collector helps bring these relations into view, his collection at the National Museum of Natural History also reminds us that all collections contain other collections, individuals and events. Specimen 125012, and its presumed field collector, the Reverend Lawes, is a case in point.

Born in Aldermaston, Berkshire, Reverend William George Lawes was a pioneering European contributor to the London Missionary Society's work in southeast New Guinea. After becoming a priest in 1860 and marrying Fanny Wickham, Lawes travelled to the island of Niue, where he served the LMS from 1861 to 1872. On 1 December 1874 he settled with his family in the then nascent settlement of Port Moresby, where he was to remain until retiring in 1906. Over his thirty-two years in New Guinea, Lawes was instrumental in the LMS' regional spread, and was a key interlocutor for the colonial government (Langmore 1989). Travelling throughout the south-eastern coast, Lawes took a vast array of photographs (Webb 1998, 2006), and either directly collected or facilitated the collection of cultural and natural history specimens (Bell 2013). Lawes devoted much of his time to understanding Motu, the language of the Motu people who occupied the immediate area of Port Moresby and the surrounding coast, and which became the dominate lingua franca of the colonial period (Dutton 1985). He published his *Grammar and Vocabulary of the Language spoken by the Motu Tribe* (Lawes 1885), and translated the New Testament into Motu in 1890.

Though relatively quiet regarding his natural history collecting in comparison to his photographic and ethnographic work, Lawes was nevertheless productive and knowledgeable (Lawes 1880). In the late 1870s, Lawes made and sent a small collection of fifty-three birds to the British Museum (Sharpe 1877/79) and another collection to the Oxford University Museum (Sclater 1893). In a widely discussed incident, he also discovered an echidna in the Port Moresby region, which he sent to London (Ramsay 1877). In his capacity as translator, Lawes accompanied the noted Scottish naturalist and merchant Andrew Goldie on some of his forays into the interior of New Guinea to carry out collecting. During these trips, Lawes shot birds alongside Goldie, and may have begun his collecting as well (Moore and Mullins 2012, 71). In his journals Lawes mentions shooting, but typically this is in reference to obtaining food, as in the following instance while travelling to Kapakapa: "Ashore after dinner with some natives from Kapaka, and went into the bush, to see if I could shoot anything good to eat. Got four spur-winged plovers and seven snipes" (King 1909, 106). Later, in Kerepunu, Lawes notes, "Out early this morning...with Aneteru shooting. Got twenty birds for eighteen shots..." (King 1909, 108). Though not detailing his collecting, passages such as this help establish Lawes' familiarity with birds, his capacity with a gun and his interaction with Pacific Island teachers, such as Aneteru, to obtain birds.

Pacific Island teachers formed the vanguard of the LMS on the Papuan coast, arriving from the Loyalty Islands (1871), Cook Islands (1872), Niue (1874), Society Islands (1878) and Samoa (1884) (Lange 2006). Some 190 Pacific Island teachers and their spouses served from 1871 to 1891, and of this number half died and eight were killed (Munro & Thornley 1996). The impact of these teachers along the Papuan coast was profound, introducing as they did a broad set of social practices and material skills (Bell 2013).

These teachers also helped facilitate the making of collections found in numerous metropolitan museums, whether they be objects obtained by members of the LMS or commercial and government agents. A letter by the Reverend James Chalmers (1841-1901) to the *Brisbane Courier* is telling. He comments, "I know a teacher collecting beetles for [Andrew Goldie], another collecting clubs, &c.; another shields, &c.; another plumes; and Mr Goldie is not the man to leave services unpaid" (1880, 5). In another instance, when visiting the New Guinea mission, the Reverend Wyatt Gill (1828-1896), a noted naturalist and pastor in the Cook Islands, received the gifts of a rose-hill parakeet, an echidna and a crocodile skin from his former Cook Islands pupils Tipoki, Maka and Pakia in 1884 (Chalmers & Gill 1885, 276-7). Not only was the region awash in natural history specimens, but most, if not all of the new residents, European and Pacific Islander alike, collected and traded them. It may very well have been that Lawes obtained some of his birds, and perhaps even specimen 125012, through this network of teachers.

While the origin of specimen 125012 will most likely remain unclear, the network that this moustached treeswift helps reveal is telling of the role of missionaries in natural history collecting in New Guinea and elsewhere. Collecting for themselves, and with the help of Europeans, Pacific Islanders and New Guineans, the specimens obtained by LMS representatives provided early glimpses of the region's incredible biodiversity. Though less examined, natural history collecting constituted an important domain of missionary activity.

It is perhaps significant that the local name of specimen 125012 was not recorded. Known by a variety of names due to the bird's wide range, Moustached Treeswifts are alternatively known as *koisereka/koisere* by Motuan speakers and *koitareke* by Koitabu speakers.[17] Restoring local names to such specimens, and assembling indigenous knowledge about them, is a critical further step in understanding the histories of missionary collections of natural history and realizing their full potential for the present.

---

17 Sebastian Haraha and Miriam Supuma graciously tapped their networks in Papua New Guinea to help identify these local names.

Slit drum, Vanuatu

Chantal Knowles

This Efate drum, now displayed in National Museums Scotland in Edinburgh, was collected by the missionary James Lawrie, who volunteered to serve for the Free Church of Scotland in the New Hebrides (modern-day Vanuatu) with his wife Margaret in 1878. Presbyterian missionaries had been established on Aneityum, Vanuatu, in 1848 with the arrival of Canadian John Geddie. By 1878 they were well established, with congregations across the southern New Hebrides, including Efate and as far north as Santo (Lawson 1994, 80). The large-scale slit drums of central Vanuatu were unique to Oceania, but their presence in the world's museums today is suggestive of their absence in the village locations for which they were originally made – a direct outcome of missionary encounters.

Although meaning and use varied from island to island, slit drums were typically assembled in groups or orchestras in a public space and added to as new drums were commissioned. Described as "sonorous ancestral figures" combining the voice and the appearance of ancestors (Fischer 1983[1932]: 28), their centrality to village architecture and ceremonial practices meant they became a focus for missionary concerns in central Vanuatu. Drums were played by men as they circled the drums in a clockwise direction – when sounded they signalled an important event and called participants to order and action.

Cylindrical in form, with a slit along its length, the drum would sound out a range of notes. Drums from this region are less obviously anthropomorphic than those found on neighbouring islands; the features of this example include the long gaping slit terminating in a circular aperture at either end, with a bored hole at the tapering top. Incised lines on the left side of the aperture, formerly highlighted with blue and red, are a more abstracted form of mouth and eyes. Speiser (1996, 348) likened them to hollowed out statues and noted that the rank of the owner was expressed in the carvings on the drums. The top-sail schooner carved in the upper portion of the drum represents a European vessel of the type used by missionaries and traders, but is likely to be associated with the attributes of the original owner.

Figure 1: Upright slit drum, Efate, Vanuatu. A.1889.37 National Museums Scotland. Courtesy of National Museums Scotland.

Missionaries in the region understood drums as religious statues and their toppling became a powerful indication of the conversion of the community to Christianity. In some cases the drums were put to new uses, literally converted following the adoption of Christianity. Rev. J. W. MacKenzie, a missionary in southern Efate, described the drums in his area:

> *We have a fence around our church of what was once their heathen gods. These gods were made from a very hard kind of a tree, and they stand a long time. They are about ten feet long, and are carved and hollowed out. They had set them up, a great many of them together, in their dancing-ground, and when struck with the fist they give a hollow sound, which is heard at a distance.* (MacKenzie quoted in Steel 1880, 233-4)

MacKenzie was perhaps more proactive than many missionaries, having sited his home and church on and adjacent to the drums. His new architecture occupied an existing sacred space, and desacralizing the drums through silencing them and integrating them into the utilitarian fence of the church complex signalled their displacement by Christianity.

The removal or displacement of objects appears to have been central to efforts to extend the evangelisation of the community, and Lawrie's published letters highlight his own efforts to remove certain artefacts and end their production. These included bamboo containers filled with earth for sorcery and sacred stones for good garden weather. He recounts the burning of a kava bowl by locals to demonstrate to him their rejection of kava consumption.

Lawrie's regular correspondence with the church in Scotland was published in their newsletter. He uses words such as "heathen", "rude" and "meagre" to describe the objects and lives of the locals but also gives detailed descriptions of local practices. This regular correspondence was a call to action, a reminder of occupations abroad as the Lawrie family relied on Scottish donations of clothing, tools and trade items to sustain their supplies. His letters had to muster and maintain the interest of the Scottish congregations. His donations to the National Museum were publicised at length in the national newspaper *The Scotsman* and amongst highlights to see was "a stone god (a water-worn stone) whose aid is invoked by natives before going to fish" (Anonymous 1889, 7).

In addition to his writings for the church and elsewhere, Lawrie was a keen photographer, and his photographs of the Vanuatu landscape and local people were commended in photographic circles (Edwards 2012, 169). When all of his writings over the years are read together, Lawrie expresses a deep interest in the region and its culture, and sympathy and warmth for Ni-Vanuatu. He expressed regular concern about population decline, chiefly resulting from contact with Europeans and successive waves of imported diseases. Over the course of his sixteen years in the region, he recognized that congregation numbers were dwindling, not always due to lack of converts or some reverting to traditional practices, but rather due to rapid population decline.

It is his published letters and photographs that are best known to Ni-Vanuatu through their exhibition in the Vanuatu Kaljoral Senta in 1998 (Adams 1998). A gift from the Australian Museum in 1980 of a smaller drum from the large grove on mainland Efate to commemorate independence resulted in the drum briefly being taken out to Mele, where it had originally stood. The relevant descendants of the lineages associated with the orchestra were able to assemble beside it.

Although based on Aneityum rather than Efate, Lawrie travelled widely round the southern islands in the *Dayspring*, the missionary schooner, not unlike the one depicted on this drum. He went to meet with congregations and support the many indigenous missionaries who were deployed across the region, but could easily have loaded items such as this slit drum on to the *Dayspring* for removal from the islands. This drum and another in the Metropolitan Museum, New York, are the largest objects collected by him and provide, in their present isolation, solitary reminders of the orchestras in which they once stood. Like the drums converted to fence posts, they are emblematic of the displacement of the old with the new, the physical manifestations of the missionary enterprise and the rejection of traditional objects as part of embracing Christian doctrine and ritual. What could be a more physical or tangible message to supporters in Scotland than the erection of a drum in their National Museum?

Acknowledgements

Tracking and tracing the history of the drums has involved the help and support of many colleagues, including Raymond Amman, Eve Haddow, Ross Irving, Christian Kauffman, Eric Kjellgren, Ken Moore and Ralph Regenvanu. Particular thanks are due to Kirk Huffman, for his help in accurately pinpointing the origin of the NMS drum, and Kylie Moloney, who created an overview of Lawrie's NMS collection and instigated much of the subsequent research.

Sorcerer's kit, Papua New Guinea

Tabitha Cadbury

In 1898, during the famous Cambridge expedition to the Torres Strait (see Herle, this volume), the anthropologist and curator Alfred Cort Haddon encountered the missionary Harry Moore Dauncey (1863-1928) on Thursday Island, off the north-east tip of Australia. The Reverend Dauncey had, by this stage, been working in Papua New Guinea (PNG) for a decade. Although Haddon recorded little in his journal of his impression of the missionary, he did note that Dauncey had given him:

> *3 shields, a number of Papuan Gulf masks – and best of all a sorcerer's kit – a basket which contains the skull of a very small crocodile, claws of a cassowary[,] various stones – bamboo receptacles and an earthen pot... if only one could find out how it was all used, it would be splendid.*[18]

The interest these two men took in what they called "sorcerer's kits" appears to have been shared, although it emanated from slightly different concerns.

Haddon returned to Britain, taking this sorcerer's kit with him, where it was subsequently joined by at least one other example at the Museum of Archaeology and Anthropology in Cambridge. Dauncey, on the other hand, continued to work in Papua New Guinea until his retirement in 1928, where he seems to have acquired another example of a "sorcerer's kit" (Figure 1), later sold to the Plymouth Museum, where it remains today (we think that it came with the rest of Dauncey's collection in either 1909 or 1923, but this particular object was not accessioned until 1983). We might assume that whereas Haddon treated his "sorceror's kit" as a scientific specimen, Dauncey would have viewed a "sorcerer's kit" as a trophy for his Christian religion. However, there was considerably more overlap than this between the outlook and interests of the two men. While Haddon was himself a member of the Congregational Church, largely responsible for sending and supporting London Missionary Society (LMS) missionaries, Dauncey had more

Figure 1. Woven bag and its contents, reputedly a sorcerer's, from the Maive District, PNG. Small net bags, tightly woven from bark or flax fibre, were used to carry personal hunting charms and amulets. Plymouth City Museum and Art Gallery: AR.1983.1220.1-14.

18 Haddon, A. C. 1898. Expedition Private Journal, p.98: Cambridge University Library Haddon Papers. Env. 1030.

than a passing interest in trying to understand local practices in Papua New Guinea, including those associated with sorcery. Is it possible to see Dauncey's "sorcerer's kit" as less of a trophy and more of a specimen, and at the same time to understand Haddon's kit as less of specimen and more of a trophy, albeit perhaps of the triumph of rational science?

The "sorcerer's kit" in the World Cultures collection at Plymouth City Museum and Art Gallery, which is the main focus for this chapter, takes the form of a net bag containing magical objects. The bag itself is plain, in two shades of natural

Figure 2. "Who is he?" This page from one of Dauncey's photograph albums shows the missionary dressing up in a local ceremonial headdress. Council for World Mission/SOAS Library: CMW/LMS/Papua New Guinea/Photographs Box 6 - File 8/14.

fibre, and was originally filled with over fifty tiny objects used as charms, now separately stored. These include pebbles, quartz crystals, pieces of coral, small animal bones and a fragment of human bone, pieces of resin and sticks, scraps of red and white trade cloth, and a crystal finely wrapped in a tiny net bag of its own.

Today, New Guinea consists of the Indonesian provinces of Papua and West Papua in the West, and Papua New Guinea (PNG) in the East. People have lived in New Guinea for over 50,000 years, but when Dauncey arrived, European rule was in its early stages. Although the first European (Dutch) settlers arrived in the west in 1828, the protectorate of British New Guinea (BNG) was only proclaimed in the eastern part of the island in 1884. Christian missionaries were often the first Europeans to settle into local communities for long periods of time, and in the process often acquired a range of items, many of which have ended up in European museum collections. We know a great deal about Dauncey from the objects, photographs and written words he left behind.[19] These tell us a lot about life in PNG at the turn of the twentieth century, as seen through a missionary's eyes.

In 1888, Dauncey sailed from Plymouth to Papua New Guinea to begin his new life as a missionary for the London Missionary Society. He came from a strongly religious family (who, like the Haddons, attended a Congregationalist church) and he stated in a letter written in 1896 and addressed from Cheshunt College in Hertfordshire, where he trained to be a missionary, that "I cannot remember the time when I had not a strong desire to engage in the foreign work".[20] Dauncey's commitment was rewarded with his first choice posting, in PNG. At the age of twenty-five, he was stationed at Port Moresby (the capital of PNG), and afterwards at the village of Delana in the Papuan Gulf, where he remained until his retirement to Bournemouth in 1928. Dauncey published a book about his life and work, *Papuan Pictures* (1913), which gives us some clues about the context in which he collected objects and the people he collected them from. He took pride in his friendly, if paternalistic, relationships with the people he was trying to convert – not just to Protestantism, but to a European way of life. In his book, Dauncey depicts himself as patient and cheerful, and the locals as needing his help.

Nevertheless, *Papuan Pictures* demonstrates a fascination with and desire to record local ways of life, as well as to transform some aspects of them. Dauncey wrote proudly of his open-mindedness in suffering some traditions to continue – such as dancing, music and local modes of dress – as long as they did not conflict with Christianity. In this, he contrasted himself to less tolerant forms of mission that insisted on wholesale eradication of local practices. There was clearly a sense of rivalry between local Catholic and Protestant missionaries, which Dauncey

19 In addition to museums, a number of other institutions hold archival material relating to Dauncey. The Royal Anthropological Institute (RAI) has over three hundred original glass plate negatives taken by Dauncey himself, as well as photographic prints and paper archives. More than sixty boxes containing Dauncey's original diaries, correspondence, reports and photograph albums are stored in the Council for World Mission's (CWM) archives. These papers give us insights into his motivations and frustrations.

20 Council for World Mission/SOAS Library (CWM/LMS/Home/Candidates Papers, 1796-1899/Box 4).

feared would confuse the local people. Despite his interest in local customs, the prevalence of sorcery in PNG appears to have been a particular concern – Dauncey devoted a whole chapter of his book to "the sorcerer". In his opinion, "if sorcerers could be banished from Papua, nearly all troubles would be banished with them. There are nominal chiefs in the villages, but their power is as nothing beside that of the sorcerer" – a power which, he says, "seems to depend upon the possession of

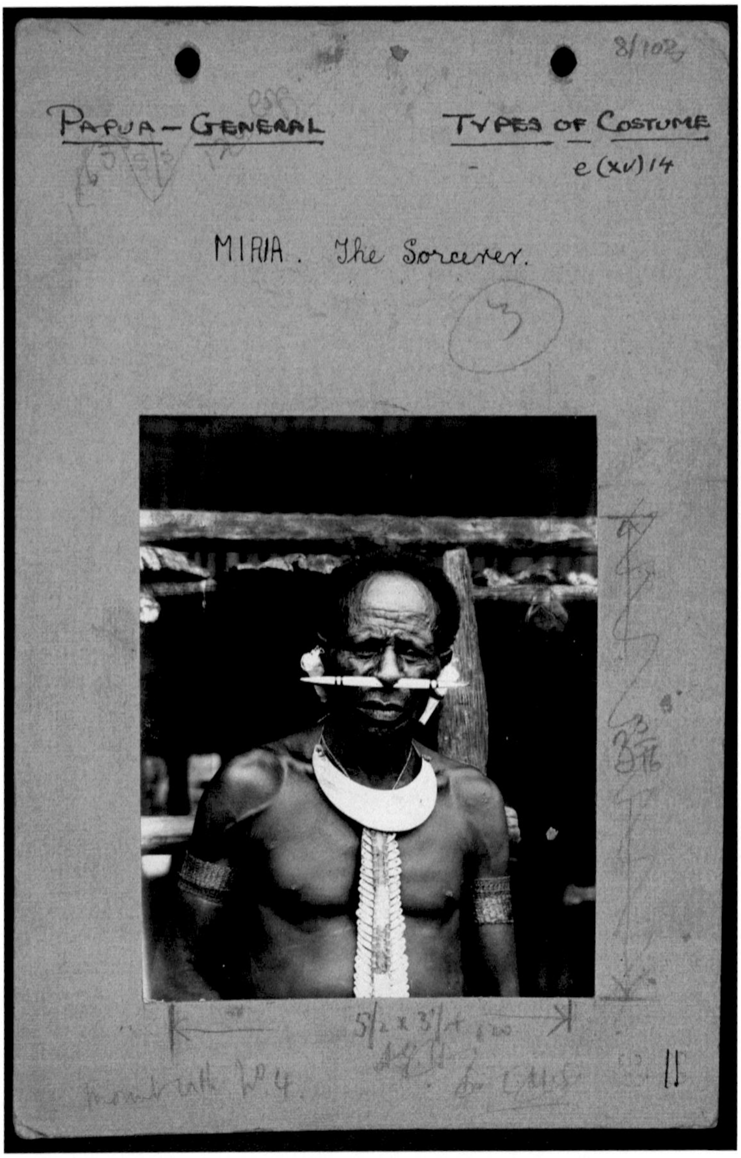

Figure 3. "Miria. The sorcerer". This page from one of Dauncey's photograph albums shows Miria, Delana's village sorcerer mentioned by Dauncey in his book, *Papuan Pictures.* **The image is marked up for publication in a missionary magazine.** Council for World Mission/SOAS Library (CMW/LMS/Papua New Guinea/ Photographs Box 6 - File 8/14).

certain charms, and these may be almost anything from a stone to a bone" (1913, 44). Dauncey describes how a typical sorcerer's kit was used: "A man is sick and a sorcerer is called in from a neighbouring village. He brings his outfit with him and, spreading the strange articles around him, begins to examine the patient. More often than not he pronounces it a case of a snake or a stone somewhere inside the patient..." and appears to remove this and with it, the sickness (1913, 50).

In much of PNG, the veneration of ancestors was, and continues to be, of considerable importance. Spiritual care may be given to the ancestors in return for their assistance in daily life, such as ensuring success in warfare, hunting, pig husbandry and gardening taro, a staple crop. Boys and men were initiated into secret aspects of oral history, religion and the ancestor cult at different stages of their lives. These initiations took place through a series of ceremonies which began in childhood and continued until each man's late twenties. For ritual specialists – like the sorcerer – this accumulation of sacred knowledge continued throughout their adult lives. Sorcerers were regarded with both awe and suspicion as their spiritual accomplishments could be used for good or for ill, to heal or to kill (1913, 51); they could act in good faith, or as charlatans. The suspicion with which Europeans regarded sorcerers, however, appears to have been universal. In his book, Dauncey comments that "there are many unsolved mysteries about the sorcerer, but all, Government officers, missionaries, and natives, vote him a nuisance" (1913, 52).

Sorcery was illegal under British colonial rule, and kits could be confiscated as part of a sorcerer's arrest. Dauncey does not refer to any particular kit in his book, but does describe how "the magistrate of the district was making a raid upon the sorcerers, and though the man escaped he left his 'kit' behind him. Amongst other things were two earthenware pots fitting the one over the other, and forming a closed vessel. Inside was a human skull" (1913, 51).

The "sorcerer's kit" now in Plymouth may have originally belonged to Miria (Figure 3), a sorcerer much discussed by Dauncey in *Papuan Pictures* (1913, 45).[21] Original documentation found with the Plymouth kit states that it is a "Sorcerer's outfit used as evidence in a court trial". Dauncey describes how ritual practitioners went to great lengths to conceal and protect their powerful objects (1913, 46-7). In one incident, Miria himself "was accused of having caused the death of a man" and "the magistrate was determined to take all his charms from him. In the end Miria told where they were hidden..." (1913, 48-9). It is tempting to think that the sorcerer's kit now at Plymouth may have been among these.

Dauncey acquired objects throughout his life and work in PNG, and sold many of these to the museum at Plymouth later in his career, in 1909 and 1923. He does not describe exactly how he collected the objects – he may have received some as gifts from the people he worked with, and obtained others through local systems of barter and exchange, since his collection contains a broad range of artefacts. We can tell from archival material that Dauncey was constantly short of money

21 This was suggested by Joshua Bell in 2007.

to do his work, so financial motivations may have been important in Dauncey's accumulation of a collection that he could later sell for money.

The museum in Plymouth is just one of several institutions where objects originally acquired by Dauncey have ended up.[22] Others include the Pitt Rivers Museum (PRM) in Oxford, the Museum of Archaeology and Anthropology (MAA) in Cambridge, the Royal Anthropological Institute (RAI) in London, the Council for World Mission's (CWM) archive at the School of Oriental and African Studies (SOAS), and the British Museum (BM). His photographs can be found at the Harvard Peabody Museum in the USA and at the Australian Museum in Sydney, while there are two masks at the National Museum of Denmark (NMD). While some material was acquired directly from Dauncey, as in the case of the thirteen objects acquired by MAA through Haddon, in other cases material was transferred between museums, such as in 1910 when Plymouth sold thirty-six objects from its Dauncey collection to the PRM.[23]

It is clear from Dauncey's writings that mission life could be tedious and difficult.[24] The lack of progress was sometimes disheartening from a missionary's point of view, as teaching assistants went home, new buildings were left to decay, and people returned to traditional forms of life. On sorcery, Dauncey comments that "the white man may work the cure, but the native leaning towards sorcery is again shown in the patient going quietly away to the sorcerer, and paying a good price to have the restoration to health approved and made secure" (1913, 160-1). Although Dauncey complained of such setbacks in his unpublished writing, he remained optimistic in public.

PNG has changed a great deal since Dauncey assembled his collection a century ago. Although it gained its independence in 1975, it remains part of the British Commonwealth. In a 2000 census, 96% of Papua New Guineans identified themselves as Christian, although many people today combine Christianity with traditional beliefs and practices. Ultimately, Dauncey's work contributed to the religious transformation of PNG, now largely a Christian country, and the sorcerer's kit at the Plymouth City Museum and Art Gallery played its part in the conversion of Papua New Guinea from "the old religion" to Christianity. It also continues to influence the ways in which we in Britain understand PNG as a place. The kit is not just a "trophy" of Christianity's triumph in PNG; its presence in the Museum draws our minds towards the very practices that Dauncey tried so hard to eradicate, and that some Christians in PNG still fear today. Objects like these have also played their part in how we see ourselves, whether by comparing ourselves favourably with those who have practiced sorcery, or by identifying with our own ancestors who similarly channelled spiritual power through material things at times, attracting for themselves accusations of witchcraft, magic and sorcery.

---

22 The physical location of these collections attests to connections between missionaries and anthropologists, collectors and museums.

23 These may have been thought of as "duplicates" because many of them – including stone tools, weapons, lime spatulas, musical instruments and personal adornments – look similar to objects still at Plymouth.

24 Dauncey was supported by his wife, Mary Ellen (née Hinton), who joined him in 1894. They had four children, three of whom survived.

Brass Necklet, Uganda

Rachel Hand

On 5 July 1902, a fairly unusual group of men arrived in Cambridge. They included Apolo Kaggwa (1864-1927), the *Katikkiro* (or prime minister) of Buganda in the British Protectorate of Uganda, his secretary Ham Mukasa (1868–1956) and their official interpreter and chaperone, Rev. Ernest Millar of the Church Missionary Society (CMS). They were in England to represent Uganda at the coronation of King Edward VII. They spent an afternoon with another CMS missionary from Uganda, John Roscoe, who was on furlough with his family in Cambridge.

Together, they went for coffee with Sir James Frazer, one of the most famous scholars in the world at the time. Roscoe had been a regular correspondent with Frazer from Uganda, supplying him with information about the Baganda for his acclaimed book on comparative religion, *The Golden Bough,* originally published in 1890 but expanded significantly in subsequent years. Frazer had donated Scottish and Asian items to the Museum of Archaeology and Anthropology, established in Cambridge in 1884, and it is possible that he influenced both Kaggwa and Roscoe to contribute to the museum's growing collection.

Kaggwa subsequently made a donation through Roscoe of sixteen items, recorded as entering the museum in 1903. They included this brass necklet (Figure 1), worn by the royal bodyguard when in the presence of the *Kabaka* (or Buganda King), as well as a number of important religious objects relating to the Bagandan deity Lubare.

During his time as a missionary in Uganda between 1884 and 1909, Roscoe set about finding out as much as he could about traditional ways of life, as they were before the influences of Europeans and Christianity. Apolo Kaggwa was vital in directing and supporting Roscoe's work, introducing him to elderly informants, enabling his visits to priests from the old temples, and supporting his collecting activities. Roscoe's book, *The Baganda: An Account of Their Native Customs and Beliefs* (1911), still seen today as the authoritative study of the Baganda, was the culmination of their collaborative work over more than two decades.

The relatively modest donation by Kaggwa in 1903 was followed by a further 700 items from Uganda, presented by Roscoe between 1904 and 1920. These included Bagandan royal relics and the remains (jawbone, umbilical cord and

Figure 1. Penannular brass necklet, E 1903.466, given to MAA by Sir Apolo Kaggwa, through the Rev. John Roscoe in 1903. Courtesy of the Museum of Archaeology and Anthropology, University of Cambridge.

genitals) and regalia (stool, leopard skin and knife) of Kibuka, the war god – acquired through Kaggwa's intervention (Roscoe 1907).[25]

Kaagwa was highly literate in Luganda, and the author of a number of books in his own right, also on the history and folklore of the Baganda. He had been an early Baganda convert to Anglicanism in the 1870s, and rose to prominence as leader of the Protestant faction in the civil wars of the Baganda (1888–1892). Under British influence, Kaggwa became *Katikkiro* in 1890 and one of the regents for the young *Kabaka*, Daudi Chwa (1896–1939), in 1897.

Mukasa's published account of their trip suggests that both he and Kaggwa had a keen interest in understanding more about the people in whose empire they found themselves. They began observing and questioning the English passengers on their habits during the sea voyage, and travelled extensively while in England (Gikandi 1998, 21, 69). They were intrigued by the animals at the Natural History Museum and the Egyptian mummies at the British Museum, but paid particular attention to the latter's Ugandan material, presented by Sir Harry Johnston (Special Commissioner for Uganda 1899 – 1902) and Roscoe himself. They also engaged in a certain amount of collecting of their own, acquiring a range of items during their tour including iron kettles, gun bores and paper samples, alongside gifts of a gold spoon, a coronation cup, pens, rifles and a printing press.

During the three days they spent in Cambridge, the group visited the University Press and University Library, noting with interest that a copy of Kaggwa's own book on the kings of Uganda was retained there (Gikandi 1998, 21). Kaggwa subsequently furthered his Cambridge connections by sending his eldest son to preparatory school nearby (Johnston 1998 [1904], 46). It is clear that while Apolo Kaggwa and Ham Mukasa were interested in studying the English in the way that they and Roscoe had together studied the customs of the Buganda, as participants in the British empire, they were also keen to find a place for themselves in the University they referred to as "the tutor of the world", responsible as it was for educating so many CMS missionaries to Uganda.[26]

By presenting traditional royal and religious objects to the Museum of Archaeology and Anthropology in Cambridge, was Kaggwa demonstrating his ability to engage with the museum as an enlightened and cultured Christian individual, an equal partner in empire and Anglicanism, rather than simply as a subject of study? Did Kaggwa understand his donations to MAA as trophies of Christianity, in the way that many missionaries, including Roscoe, understood certain items as symbols of their evangelising success? Or was it the museum itself, and the part he contributed to establishing its collections, that was a greater trophy for Sir Apolo Kaggwa KCMG MBE?

---

25 In 1961, a former Cambridge student, Abubaker Kakyama Mayanja, the Ugandan Minister of Education, asked for the return or loan of Kibuka's relics (A. K. Mayanja, 20 October 1961. "Letter to the Vice Chancellor, University of Cambridge." *Museum of Archaeology and Anthropology Archives*, AA4/5/15). The relics were returned and used to celebrate Ugandan Independence in October 1962, then housed in the Uganda National Museum in Kampala.

26 These included Harry Leakey (Peterhouse College), Sir Albert Cook (Trinity College) and George Pilkington (Pembroke College).

A Bird of the Net, Solomon Islands

Ben Burt

This wooden bird from the Lau area of Malaita, Solomon Islands, came to the British Museum from the collection of Harry Beasley, who purchased it in 1931, and noted its history in his catalogue:

> *This was the TINDALO emblem of the people of FERA-SI-BOA, a fishing tribe of N. Mala and was presented to the Rev. A. I. Hopkins of the Melanesian Mission by Chief KAILAFA in 1905. It was preserved in the Chief's canoe house, suspended over the altar, and when presented was black with soot. The Rev. Hopkins said that the culture of these people was not very high and that this piece was probably the product of another locality.*[27]

Beasley amassed a huge worldwide collection of artefacts in his Cranmore Museum and the bird was among those given to the British Museum by his widow in 1944. Many of the ones from the Solomons were sent by his missionary contacts, with local provenances which Beasley noted in his catalogues, but when missionaries collected artefacts on their own account, they seldom showed such interest in their identities. The Anglican Melanesian Mission to which Reverend Arthur I. Hopkins belonged received great quantities of artefacts from Solomon Islands from the late nineteenth to mid-twentieth centuries, mostly solicited as gifts from local congregations. These were contributed for sale to raise funds for the Mission, or presented to build relationships with missionaries in appreciation of their services in mediating with God and the colonial authorities, as recorded by Hopkins on several occasions.[28] The British branch of the Melanesian Mission held a collection of artefacts obtained in this way which it used for advertising its work. This included about 1,450 artefacts from Solomon Islands when it was dispersed in 1991, but only about fifty were labelled as such, let alone with the level of detail recorded for Hopkins' bird (Burt 1991).

Figure 1. The British Museum's bird of the net (BM Oc1944,02.1332). Courtesy of the Trustees of the British Museum.

27 Ledger: British Museum Archive. See British Museum online catalogue under Oc.1944,02.1332 (http://www.britishmuseum.org/research/collection_online/collection_object_details.aspx?objectId=495539&partId=1&searchText=bird+hopkins&page=1, accessed August 2014).

28 *Southern Cross Log: the Journal of the Melanesian Mission*, 1905, 9; 1906, 39.

The failure of the Melanesian Mission to document its collections may seem surprising considering the particular interest some of its members took in the culture of the people they were working with. One, Robert Codrington, wrote the first, still influential, ethnography of Melanesia (1891); another, Charles Fox, wrote an ethnography of Makira island (1924), and Walter Ivens took time to research and write two very detailed ethnographies of districts of Malaita, of Sa'a in the south (1927) and of Lau (1930), where Hopkins obtained the bird. However, these books seldom identify specific artefacts, including those belonging to Ivens, which came to the British Museum after his death with no more information than some vaguely captioned illustrations in his books on Sa'a (see Burt 2013). Interest in local culture served the greater purpose of Christian evangelism and did not extend to the curio collector's or museum curator's concern for artefact provenances. Hopkins' bird was unusual in being identified, not only by time and place but also by persons and circumstances, only because of its special significance to him in terms of his mission.

Beasley's characteristically thorough catalogue entry gives no more than a glimpse of the story behind this object, but in retirement in 1934 Hopkins wrote about it in his autobiography. Unlike his rather vague and dull book, *In the Isles of King Solomon* (1928), this informative memoir remained a typescript in the Melanesian Mission archives until it was published online in 2005 (Hopkins 1934). It contains not only a more detailed account of how he obtained the bird, but also outlines his long-term relationship with the man who gave it to him, Kaialafa, which was of vital importance to his mission in Lau and north Malaita. What it does not explain is why the bird was so important to the people of Lau for, unlike his colleague Ivens, Hopkins showed little interest in the culture of Malaita beyond its implications for the Christian church. It was not until the 1960s that the significance of such birds became known beyond Lau.

Hopkins was the first resident Anglican missionary in north Malaita when he arrived in 1902 at Ngorengorefou, a settlement on the shore of the lagoon where the Lau sea people lived on small artificial islands. This small Christian community had been founded a year or two previously by a group of ten Malaitan men who had returned as converts from labour migration to Fiji and Queensland. They were continually harassed by their neighbours of both the inland and the offshore islands, and their leader Alfred Amasia had just been killed (see Burt 2002). Hopkins himself was under the same threat from those who resented the increasing influence of 'Whitemen' (*Ara'ikwao*), their political and commercial interests, and their Christian allies. However, the Christians also had relatives and friends among the inland communities and the sea people of the lagoon, in particular Kaialafa as chief of the offshore island of Ferasubua. Kaialafa and his men stood off several attempts by parties and individuals to kill Hopkins, which might have destroyed the Christian settlement entirely, and they helped erect a solid protective stockade around Ngorengorefou, within which Hopkins later had a substantial house built by a Melanesian Mission carpenter.

Figure 2. Kaialafa and the sanctum house where he kept the bird would have looked very like this, photographed on Ferasubua island by John W. Beattie in 1906. (Beattie 522, BM Oc,B114-78). Courtesy of the Trustees of the British Museum.

Exactly why Kaialafa was such a strong supporter of the Christians, when he showed no inclination to join the church himself, Hopkins did not say. According to Ivens, who helped introduce Hopkins to Ngorengorefou, Kaialafa was chief as head of the senior lineage of Ferasubua (Ivens 1930, 63-4). He was over seventy in 1900, so already mature when the Lau people first encountered 'Whitemen' in the 1860s. Perhaps he was astute enough to recognise the inevitable consequences of the increasing colonial intrusion which he had witnessed over his long lifetime. When Hopkins arrived, Malaitans had been dealing with Whitemen for more than a generation, sending men to work on plantations overseas to obtain valuable metal tools, firearms and imported luxuries such as tobacco. The most powerful leader in Lau, Kwaisulia of Adagege island, had participated in this labour trade from its beginnings in the 1870s and gained influence as a broker with recruiters and warships (Corris 1970). He attempted to control the Christians of Ngorengorefou and persecuted them when they resisted his authority, and Hopkins too resisted Kwaisulia's patronage because he disapproved of him providing captives as recruits and feud victims. But the power of leaders like Kwaisulia was limited by the growing colonial presence. While the Malaita inland was still secure from attack, the sea people, living on small offshore islands in tension with their inland neighbours, recognised their vulnerability to the warships which patrolled Malaita. Ngongosila island to the south, well known to the people of Lau, had been bombarded and burned in 1882 in retaliation for the sinking of a recruiting ship. In 1902, about a month before Hopkins arrival, HMS *Sparrow* had burned Oru island to the north, compelled Kwaisulia to hand over the killers of Amasia, and then sacked Ngongosila again for the killing of a Christian (Burt 1994, 114-5; Burt 2002). Hopkins' own authority depended not only on his religious services to Christians at Ngorengorefou and around the coast, who were working for a transformation of Malaitan society, but also on the manifest support of the visiting warships, now directed by the colonial government from its base at Tulagi in nearby Gela.

Hopkins' friendship must have been of political value to Kaialafa, no doubt in resisting the encroaching power of Kwaisulia. Perhaps he really liked Hopkins and approved the message of peace preached by the Christians, even as he remained bound by obligations to his ancestral ghosts and their congregation of descendants, but Hopkins lacked the sensitivity to explore such possibilities in his autobiography. Despite his evident dedication to the people of Malaita during more than ten years of service there, enduring the physical and emotional stress of touring the island, of sickness and separation from his own kind, while gaining the loyalty of his local congregations and colleagues, Hopkins did not show any deep interest in their culture. He was focused on Christian conversion as part of the colonial advancement of civilisation and showed none of the curiosity of his colleague Walter Ivens, who would surely have investigated the significance of the bird rather than dismissing its owners as too low in culture to have made it.

The significance of the bird for Hopkins was implied in the full account in his autobiography (1934, 30):

> *The end of July 1903 was marked by my first baptism at Gnore Fou. ... It was just after this baptism* [not in 1905 as recorded by Beasley] *that Kailafa of Fera-si-boa manifested his real friendship in rather a striking way. I had heard of and coveted an "agalo" sacred image, which was stored in his hut at Fera-si-boa. Its day of power was waning but it was still of a considerable repute. Anyway the older men were very apprehensive about its proper treatment. I suggested that they should give it to me to hang in my hut as a visible proof of their friendship. Rather a big request. On a certain Tuesday early in July I returned in triumph with it in my possession. Kailafa the chief and its protector in handing it over to me said "It's a most sacred object, but I can't refuse you anything". The Gnore Fou people's attitude and that of numerous bush visitors was "Has he really given you that!" This sacred object "doo abu" was a heavy block of red wood carved into the shape of bird with a fish above and much inlaid with mother of pearl* [actually coneshell]. *It was black with smoke as its shrine was the roof of Kailafa's hut. For a week at least there was a procession of visits to see it in its new abode, cleaned up, in my hut. I suppose they speculated as to how it would settle there, would it be peaceable, or would it be wrath with Gnore Fou or Fera-si-boa? The white man himself they would imagine would get off scot free, but what of its "adherents", what of its present harbourers? Some of the disgruntled old folks at Fera-si-boa were very alarmed and expected calamities. There were mutterings "school* [mission] *no good".*

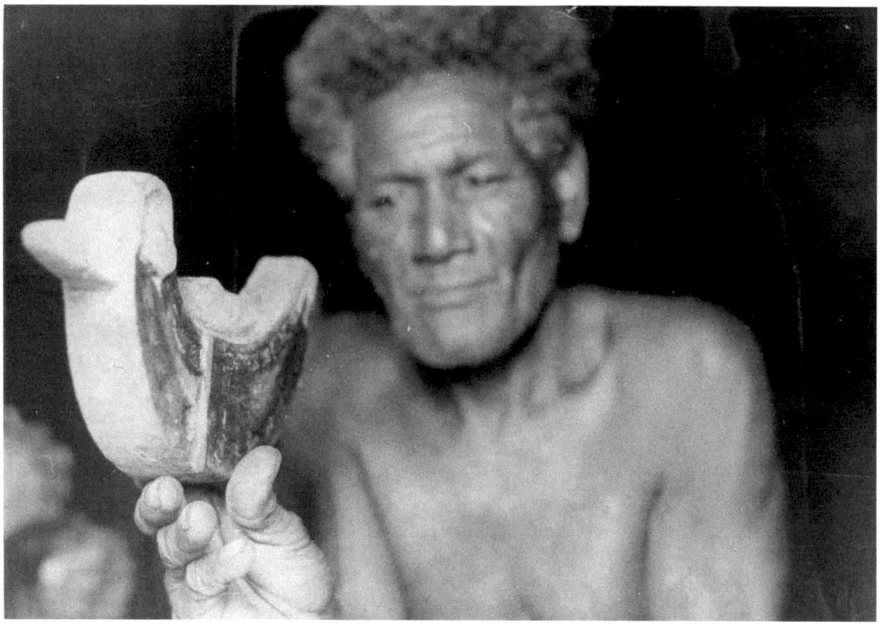

Figure 3. Kunua of Foueda island with one of his old birds of the net in 1968 (Pierre Maranda photo 0865). Courtesy of Pierre Maranda.

As it happens, Ivens did not describe such birds in his detailed ethnography of Lau, and it was not until the 1960s that anthropologist Pierre Maranda noted them while researching with one of the last Lau communities to maintain their ancestral religion against the generations of evangelism following Hopkins' presence. These people still depended on the ghosts of their ancestors, following their rules of tabu (Pijin *tambu*) and making prayers and offerings to them for spiritual support and protection. Ivens did document how their great seine nets, up to two hundred yards long and twenty feet deep, were dedicated to ancestral ghosts and protected as tabu from contact with women, which would defile them and make them ineffective. Each was owned by a chief, who preserved it both materially and spiritually by storing it over the hearth in his sanctum house in the men's area of the island, where it remained when no longer in use (Ivens 1930). Maranda found that, when large quantities of fish were required by a local clan for a festival honouring all their ancestors, to which relatives and neighbours were invited for a prestigious major celebration, a special net (*furai gigilo'a*) was used, of coconut fibre instead of bark twine. Tied to its head was a special 'bird of the net' float (*manu ana furai*) in the form of a seagull, to lead the net towards the shoals of fish. This net was even more tabu than an ordinary one and was used only once before being stored away in the chief's sanctum house, with its bird float. Maranda photographed several birds of the net kept by priest and artesan Kunua of Foueda island in his sanctum, none quite as large and impressive as Kaialafa's, and of softwood with pearlshell inlay rather than hardwood with coneshell, but similar in style. Such floats were used by other sea people as far away as Makira (see Edge-Partington 1890-8, 34), but whether they served exactly the same purpose is not recorded.

Profaning such a tabu object by exposing it to public view, and especially to contact with women, risked offending the ghosts, leading to sickness, misfortune and death. This was why Hopkins was told it was *agalo*, meaning it had spiritual agency, like an ancestral ghost (*tindalo*, as mentioned by Beasley, being the Gela equivalent often used by Anglican missionaries). Giving it to a Christian, known deliberately to flout the rules separating men and ghosts from women, would have seemed very risky to Kaialafa and his clan congregation, whose ancestors would afflict them if they were offended. Perhaps Kaialafa prayed to them for special dispensation to normalise the bird, or trusted that the power of God would neutralise the power of tabu. In any case, the gift to Hopkins was evidently one of those small events which progressively undermined faith in the ancestral ghosts by challenging their coercive power. If Hopkins understood nothing else about the bird which Kaialafa gave him, he evidently appreciated that he had gained a trophy for his Christian mission.

Acknowledgements

Thanks to Pierre Maranda for information on the bird of the net, now on the British Museum database, and for the photograph of Kunua.

Interview

François Wadra and Julie Adams

François Wadra is a Kanak archaeologist from Maré, one of the Loyalty Islands that lie off the coast of New Caledonia. In 2008 he came to London to participate in a research project working with Julie Adams at the British Museum. Since then, they have been working together tracing collections of Kanak objects in UK museums. In 2013, Wadra came to the UK to work with Adams on the Pacific Presences research project, based at the Museum of Archaeology and Anthropology, Cambridge. The two visited museums in London, Amsterdam, Leiden and Paris, where this interview was conducted on 1 November 2013.

JA: When people think about the work of missionaries, they often have a rather simplistic notion of Europeans travelling to distant parts of the world to convert local people. But the history of the missions in the Loyalty Islands is much more complex, isn't it?

FW: Yes, the first missionaries in my islands were actually Polynesians. When the London Missionary Society came from England and was anchored offshore in a big boat, rather than come ashore themselves they sent Polynesian pastors in canoes to check out if our people were ready to receive their religion. It was in 1841 when they landed in the north east of my island, Maré. In fact, a small piece of the canoe that the Polynesian pastors arrived in still survives; people have kept it to remember the arrival of the missionaries. The Polynesians worked first on Maré, but word quickly spread. When people on the next island, Lifou, heard about the advantages of having missionaries, they wanted them in their island too. When I say advantages I mean not just access to European goods but also a kind of prestige that came from having an association with Europeans. So the main mission base moved to Lifou. Later my great-grandfather became a missionary himself. He was trained in New Zealand and worked converting people in Papua New Guinea. So you see, nothing is straightforward.

JA: Although the early missionaries on the Loyalty Islands were from the London Missionary Society, on the main island it was the French Catholic missions that eventually came to dominate [a group of Marists established the first mission

Figure 1. François Wadra in Manchester Museum, examining a headdress (O.06206) made from parrot feathers collected by the missionaries James and Emma Hadfield. Photograph by Julie Adams, 2013.

Figure 2. Monument to the arrival of the London Missionary Society on the island of Maré.
Photograph by Julie Adams, 2009.

at Balade, on the north-east coast, in 1843. This ended with the mission being destroyed by local people angry at the introduction of European diseases as well as suffering from drought and starvation. When French missionaries returned in 1851, they enlisted the support of the military to help them succeed.] By the time you were growing up and being educated, was their influence still strong? Did you have direct experience of missionaries?

FW: Yes, definitely. Originally all the schools were run by missionaries. They taught people how to behave, how to respect people, how to read the Bible and write. The French system of education came later. I went to a mission school, and while the teachers themselves were not missionaries, it was a school funded by the mission. I remember that we were not allowed to speak our language; we had to speak French. Even our parents supported this because they thought that if you knew how to speak French then you were *somebody*. I remember very clearly my father saying, "we don't want to be the only ones left just speaking our language, we need to speak French too". Today, most young kids only speak French. Even if they speak the same local language, they talk to one another in French.

JA: So what would happen to you at school, if you were caught speaking your own language?

FW: Well, we were punished actually. I remember when I just started school I was really scared; scared even to hold a pen. Once, my friend and I were tied up to a pole while everyone else went to lunch because they wanted us to speak French.

Luckily my father was a teacher and he was interested in Kanak culture and history. Sometimes in the night, when I was about six or seven, he would wake me up to listen to the old people talking. He would say, "listen to what that old woman is saying, it is important". That is what helped me become an archaeologist I think. Forty years later, I still remember the old stories and they help me a lot.

JA: When I visited Maré with you in 2009, I was struck by how the landscape of your village still carries a visual reminder of the arrival of the missionaries. Do you remember how you showed me the small raised mound in the central clearing, not far from the entrance to the church, where people had brought their traditional objects to be burned?

FW: Yes, that is in the centre of my village. The burning of our traditional objects was a sign intended for the missionaries to think that we had accepted Christianity. The local chief at the time was being pressured by the missionaries to help persuade people to convert. The chief was not sure what to do, so he called upon his most powerful priest, a man who was known to perform what you might call now "black magic". He said to him: "if you are so powerful, use your skills to strike down and kill these missionaries and destroy their new religion". The priest tried but he couldn't do it, so the chief accepted Christianity. That's how it happened. The chief and the missionaries together called on everyone to bring their powerful objects, such as carved figures and things associated with magic, to the centre of the village where they were piled up and burned. Everyone knows where that place is and they don't go near it, even today.

JA: In the work that we have been doing together, tracing collections of Kanak objects in British museums, one of the largest and most important collections was made by James and Emma Hadfield of the London Missionary Society. They lived in the Loyalty Islands for over forty years [1878–1920], during which time Emma amassed a vast collection of objects, of which over one hundred are now housed in various institutions such as the British Museum, the Pitt Rivers Museum, National Museums Scotland, the Manchester Museum and the Horniman Museum. Did the scale of the Hadfield collection surprise you, and what did you make of the objects she acquired?

FW: I was surprised in the sense that we really don't have the chance to see these things at home any more. You see, people know that objects have survived, but they don't know where they are. They know their history, but the actual objects are missing. In the Islands each clan has its own objects and power – we say "magic" – and so I am surprised when I find myself in front of these objects overseas. I ask myself, "do I have the right to hold this?" If this object was at home, I know I wouldn't even be allowed to touch it. But the museum is a different kind of space, so I have the chance to touch them – but it is a big responsibility. It is clear in my mind that I don't have the right to use their power. I just record the information and take photographs so that I can show people when I go home. The important thing is, at least I can tell people I have seen these things and I can give them the information. Although the object itself is here, the spirit of the object is still with those people back home.

JA: What do you think was Emma Hadfield's motivation for making this collection?

FW: I think she was trying to understand the people she was living with through the objects they used. She wrote a book – *Among the Natives of the Loyalty Group* (1920) – and I suppose she was trying to learn about our culture. Maybe she should have tried to understand how people lived through the people themselves, rather than the objects, because what she wrote in the book is actually quite superficial. Of course, maybe she just liked some of the beautiful objects and wanted to keep them, although she actually sold a lot of them to make money for the mission. So perhaps that was her real reason. I am not scared of saying it because we have seen it: when we were at the Horniman Museum we learned that she sold one object for £10 when at that time £10 was a lot of money. So maybe it was about the money, I don't know. Sometimes when I visit museums to see objects from my islands, I have a feeling that in the end I will get to know more about the collectors than the history of the objects themselves, which is a shame. Exhibition labels often tell you who collected the object, but I say: "so what?" What I want to know is: who made these objects? How were they made? Which ceremonies were they used in? That is what Kanak people want to know.

JA: Occasionally, we come across an object that you are completely unfamiliar with, such as recently when we visited Manchester Museum and saw a beautiful feather headdress that had been collected by Emma Hadfield. However, as it is the only one we have ever seen, we were unsure what to make of it or how it might have been used. Missionaries rarely recorded the circumstances under which they acquired specific objects – this is one of the big challenges of working with museum collections, isn't it?

FW: Yes, this has a big impact on us today. Because the generation that came after the missionaries didn't have direct contact with the objects and the objects weren't in contact with the environment or space where they belonged, so there is a kind of gap. Now, when we are trying to reconnect these objects in museums with Kanak people, we don't have all the necessary information.

You can make certain assumptions about an object like this headdress because it is made from parrot feathers, which are rare in New Caledonia, and would have been used in high-status ornaments. Also, you can tell from the very fine fibre work that it would have taken a long time to make, so it was probably worn at an important ceremony, perhaps a wedding (see Figure 3). But we don't know. To understand an object you need to know its context. I always say that an object is standing in for a human being when it is used in a ceremony. Had Emma Hadfield recorded this kind of information, we would know the circumstances in which this headdress was worn or presented. Instead, we have to imagine a life for this object because we don't know its individual history.

Figure 3. The parrot feather headdress, now in the collections of Manchester Museum. Photograph courtesy of Manchester Museum.

JA: When we find rare objects like this headdress, it is really just the first step on a long journey to try and imagine the life it may have led up to the point when it was collected by a missionary. Is this why you put so many pictures of your work on Facebook, so that people in New Caledonia can immediately begin discussing these objects?

FW: Well we are now in the 21st century! We are given all the means of communication, so the reason I am putting them up there is that I want to share as much as I can. So that young kids will know about them, but also for the older people who have heard stories about these objects and can immediately post something back on Facebook – perhaps new information or clues. I am not interested in keeping these things for myself: it is my responsibility to share. This work is just the beginning of the discussion.

Some museum people say that it isn't possible for objects to be returned to where they came from because the connection has been lost, but I don't agree. A person isn't an isolated individual: he belongs to a group. So if you bring back information about an object from the Loyalty Islands and you know roughly where it was collected, people will know straight away which clan it comes from. All this doesn't mean that I think objects should come back to the islands, however. We need to have the correct conditions to preserve them and take care of them. The museum may be the best place for that. But don't tell me that it isn't possible to tell from which clan an object has come – I don't agree with that argument. Although the missionaries took these things away with them and brought them to England, the spirit of the objects stayed in the Islands. Of that I am sure.

Part Two

Relics?

David Livingstone's Magic Lantern, United Kingdom

T. Jack Thompson

In September 1853 David Livingstone was at Linyanti in what is now northern Botswana, preparing to set out towards Loanda, on the westward leg of what became his epic Trans-African journey, which lasted from 1852 to 1856 and saw him reach both the west and east coasts of Africa. He had begun the journey originally in Cape Town, and then, after a delay at the mission station of Kuruman to repair a broken wheel on his ox-wagon, he had pushed north (Ross 2002, 79). By the time he reached Linyanti he had decided (as we would say today) to "downsize": to leave many of his goods with the Makololo chief Sekeletu and take only a few boxes with him. Among his list of what he took, he comments that "a fourth box contained a magic lantern, which we found of much use" (Livingstone 1857, 230). Given the limited amount of goods he had decided to take with him, and the fact that he had only twenty-seven men in his party, the decision to take the magic lantern (and the fuel necessary to work it) is a clear indication of just how important it was to him.

The magic lantern was not, of course, a new technology in the mid-nineteenth century. Indeed, it had existed in various forms and with various means of illumination from the seventeenth century (Robinson *et al.* 2001, 318; Thompson 2012, 208-10). What was significant about Livingstone's use of the medium at this time was the fact that he carried it with him on a major expedition into the interior of Africa and used it as a means of Christian evangelization. Livingstone's magic lantern can now be seen at the David Livingstone Centre in Blantyre, Scotland.

Livingstone did not actually set out from Linyanti until November 1853. On January 1854, when he was among the Barotse of Masiko, he reported:

> *We regaled our friends with the magic lantern by night, and, in order to make the thing of use to all, we removed our camp up to the village of Nyamoana. This is a good means of arresting the attention and conveying important facts to the minds of these people.* (Livingstone 1857, 278)

Figure 1. David Livingstone's magic lantern. Image courtesy of the Livingstone Centre, Blantyre, Scotland.

Shortly afterwards, Livingstone recounts a rather more startling incident which occurred at the village of the Balonda chief Shinte. He was giving another magic lantern slide show, and was telling the Biblical story of Abraham's willingness to sacrifice his son Isaac:

> *The uplifted knife was in the act of striking the lad; the Balonda men remarked that the picture was much more like a god than the things of wood and clay they worshipped... The ladies listened with silent awe; but when I moved the slide, the uplifted dagger moving towards them, they thought it was to be sheathed in their bodies instead of Isaac's. "Mother! Mother!" all shouted at once, and off they rushed helter-skelter, tumbling pell-mell over each other, and over the little idol-huts and tobacco-bushes: we could not get one of them back again.* (Livingstone 1857, 298)

Livingstone goes on to point out that after each slide show, he made an effort to explain to people how the machine worked, "so that no one should imagine that there was aught supernatural in it" (Livingstone 1857, 298). Yet, given the strangeness of the equipment, and the often startling and realistic results it produced, it is not surprising that it should have led to such emotional reactions on occasion. However, it seems not always to have been so, for Livingstone was to comment, "This is the only means of instruction I was ever pressed to repeat" (Livingstone 1857, 299). Clearly, whether through fascination or fear, the magic lantern made a big impression.

As the century drew towards its close, the missionary use of the magic lantern in Africa became much more common. There were several reasons for this. First, as missionary presence increased and grew more settled around central mission stations, equipment such as the magic lantern became easier to use and maintain. Secondly the development of the dry plate silver gelatin process led to more photographs being turned into slides for the magic lantern. Thirdly, the general growth in the popularity of the magic lantern in Europe led to the emergence of several major commercial firms producing professional photographic studies for the magic lantern by the thousand, and created a ready pool of visual material with which missionaries could educate and evangelise their audiences.

In 1880, at the Scottish mission station of Bandawe in what is now northern Malawi – a place which Livingstone himself had visited in 1861 – the mission journal recorded that during a visit of a delegation of the Ngoni people from the hills:

> *We showed them some pictures of battles, a regiment on the march, a photo of the Zulu king now caught,*[29] *numerous forts on the Mediterranean and an entertainment with the magic lantern. We impressed upon them the necessity of taking some steps in the way of improvement.*[30]

---

29 This is a reference to King Cetshwayo, captured by the British on 28 August 1879 at the end of the Anglo-Zulu war.

30 *Bandawe Journal* 16 January 1880. Livingstonia Papers, Ms. 7910. Edinburgh: National Library of Scotland.

This two-pronged approach produced both a plethora of Biblical stories on magic lantern slides, but also sets such as "Wonders of the World", allowing European missionaries to impress their converts with what they regarded as the technological marvels of Western civilisation.

As a counter-balance to the use of the magic lantern in Africa, there was also a huge expansion in the use of the lantern slide show as a means for British missionaries to share the nature of their work with audiences at home, to encourage both financial support and missionary recruitment. Perhaps inevitably, however, such slide shows also produced stereotypes of Africa and Africans, some of which have persisted until today. Many thousands of such missionary magic lantern slides are still in existence in museums and church offices throughout Britain.[31] It is much more difficult to locate slide sets in Africa, though some do exist, such as the more than 750 slides in the Livingstonia Museum in northern Malawi (Thompson 2012, 214-24). The Livingstonia Mission was founded in memory of Livingstone just two years after his death, and its large collection of magic lantern slides reminds us of his pioneering work in this area – as does his own magic lantern in Blantyre.

31 See Mundus Gateway (www.mundus.ac.uk).

Wood image, Fiji

Steven Hooper

In August 1863, the Reverend Thomas Baker, later to become famous as the only European missionary to be killed in Fiji (see Buadromo and Igglesden, this volume), visited the island of Viwa in the Yasawa Islands, northwest of Viti Levu (not to be confused with the small island of Viwa, the Methodist mission station off south-eastern Viti Levu). In his diary entry for 7 August, Baker recounted:

> *I then prepared my offering, and went ashore, where I found abundance of food prepared for me and my men and crew. I spent the day in conversing with the people from house to house, during which time I purchased two human figures or images, being the heads of certain posts in the heathen temple. We sawed their heads of [sic] in the sight of all the people, giving as payment two large knives which were greatly prized by the owners. Perhaps these images had not been worshipped, but when an individual was clubbed and taken in war, they would take and present him before the said images. These now form a very nice, though rude, piece of furniture for my study… [A]fter presenting a whales tooth (Fijian custom) I exhorted them to become Christian, which was followed up by an appeal from the Yasawa Chief in their own dialect. Then they received the offering, and called themselves "Lotu" Christian.*[32]

One of the images recently appeared at a Paris auction (Christie's, 10 December 2013, where it was seen by the author), having found its way there from Baker's study via his daughter Clara Nui, her descendants and an art dealer in Australia. Baker's status as the only European missionary to have been killed in Fiji has made this image into a contact relic – the personal possession of the martyr. Of course, sculptures of this kind can have multiple identities, and Baker himself was uncertain about the status of the images when he acquired them. He appears to follow the view of Reverend Thomas Williams, that images were not "idols" to be worshipped. Williams wrote in 1849, after nine years' residence in different parts of Fiji, that he had "come to the conclusion that nothing of this kind is worshipped

Figure 1. The upper part of an image, collected by Reverend Thomas Baker at Viwa, Yasawa Islands, Fiji on 7 August 1863. Wood, h. 30cm. Sold at Christie's, Paris, 10 December 2013. Photograph by Steven Hooper.

32 Baker, T. 1850-66. "Baker, Rev Thomas, Diary Aug 1850 – July 1866", 171-2. Typescript. State Library of New South Wales, Mitchell Library, Sydney: MLM.O.M 128, CY3527.

by the Feejeeans" (Williams 1931, 68). In his well-known book, *Fiji and the Fijians*, which Baker had certainly read, Williams noted (1858, 216): "Idolatry – in the strict sense of the term – the Fijian seems to have never known; for he makes no attempt to fashion material representations of his gods". Also, Baker's observation about sacrificial victims being presented before the images may not be what he was actually told at Viwa, but was a view in general circulation about such consecration rites, based on the reports of earlier missionaries, including Williams (1858, 54). It seems likely that pre-Christian images of this kind played a similar role to chiefs in ritual procedures – as vehicles for and embodiments of divine ancestral presence. Whether they were "idols" depends on one's definition of worship. Hocart's view was that "the true religion of the Fijians is the service of the chiefs" (1952, 26). House and temple posts made of tropical hardwoods, especially *vesi* (*Intsia bijuga*), were considered equivalent to the bodies of chiefs; in the honorific vocabulary of eastern Fiji a high chief is still referred to as "*turaga duru vesi*" – "chief *vesi* post". To find temple posts made of tropical hardwood in the form of a figure, most likely connected to founding ancestors who still exerted influence in mundane affairs, is not therefore surprising, though they are relatively rare in Fiji.

There can be little doubt that this image is one of the two mentioned by Baker in 1863. The sculpture, 30cm high, has a flat-topped head with a triangular-shaped face that looks slightly downwards. The neck emerges from a roughly cylindrical post that has been shaped to form shoulders, upper arms and chest. Baker refers to it as an image or human figure, whose head was sawn off, so it is likely that at least the full torso was originally present. There is no indication of breasts, so it probably represents a male. The wood, of uncertain species, is extremely heavy and roughly faceted, but with a rich dark patina, probably produced by a combination of rubbing with oil, soot from temple fires and polishing when in the Baker family's possession. There are no directly comparable images in the corpus published by Larsson (1960), but most of those, as far as is known, were collected in eastern Fiji, Vanua Levu and Viti Levu. No other documented images from the Yasawa Islands are known, so this image may exhibit a distinctive local style. It does not appear to have been a structural part of the temple building; the fact that the top was easily sawn off means that the post was probably free-standing.

Relic, ancestor image, trophy for Baker's study? With some prescience, in 1843 Thomas Williams also used the expression "work of art" for a similarly roughly carved figure from Somosomo in north-eastern Fiji. He wrote: "That it ever was really worshipped is ... a very doubtful matter. It is not unlikely that it may be or may have been esteemed as a 'work of art' – an indication that, had its maker been better taught, and supplied with better tools, he might have become a tolerable carver" (Williams 1931, 67). This somewhat begrudging compliment was founded on respect for a fellow woodworker; Williams himself was a trained carpenter/joiner and would have appreciated the skill involved. Christie's certainly presented this image as a work of art in their catalogue, comparing it to a sculpture by Picasso. It has also become a commodity. To the newly converted community in the Yasawas in 1863, its exchange value was a large metal knife, hard to obtain and doubtless then of great local value. At the Paris auction it fetched €433,500. *Autres temps, autres mœurs.* Its price was certainly influenced by its new status as a relic (Hooper 2014), not just of pre-Christian Fijian religion, but as a contact relic of the cannibalised martyr Thomas Baker, adding an extra frisson to its provenance in the catalogue. I expect people are now looking for the other one.

The remains of Mr. Baker's boots recovered from near where he was murdered years after the event.
Reverend Thomas Baker's ordination

Thomas Baker's Shoes, Fiji

Sagale Buadromo and Katrina Talei Igglesden

In the Fiji Museum lie the remains of leather boots formerly belonging to Reverend Thomas Baker, who worked as a missionary in Fiji from 1859 to 1867 (Figure 1). The shoes are displayed amongst articles which supposedly aided in his killing and consumption in the Navosa highlands of western Viti Levu in 1867, such as a flesh fork, a cup and bowl for the ceremonial drinking of *yaqona* (a drink made of the roots and stems of the pepper bush *Piper methysticum*) and a presentation whale's tooth (*tabua*). The accompanying label states: "The remains of Mr Baker's boots recovered from near where he was murdered years after the event". This display case was curated by Fergus Clunie and Brenda Knuckey in the mid-1980s as part of the Museum's History Gallery. It has changed little since this time, with the exception of Baker's Bible being added in the early 1990s. All objects in the case were donated to the Museum by the Methodist Church of Fiji & Rotuma, along with other notable objects, such as the printing press which printed the first Fijian Bibles, and a clay lamp, using coconut oil as fuel and a small twisted *masi* (barkcloth) wick. Before the Methodist Church donated these objects to the Fiji Museum, they were housed in the Reverend Baker Memorial Hall in Davuilevu (Figure 2).

As the only European missionary to be killed and cannibalised in Fiji, the story of Baker's death, as told by the two students who survived the attack, remains one of the most notorious events in Fijian Methodist history (Tomlinson 2012, 222). On 20 July 1867, Reverend Baker, together with Fijian minister Setareki Seileka and eight missionary students, reached the village of Nagagadelavatu in the island's mountainous interior, an area which so far had resisted Christian conversion. As the appointed Methodist minister for the interior, Baker was travelling through the area on his way to Vuda in the Western Division. At Nagagadelavatu, he offered a *tabua* (presentation whale's tooth) to Nawawabalavu, the chief of the village, a gift ensuring safe passage which he presented in all the villages he visited. However, according to church documents, a Naitasiri chief opposed to Christianity subsequently offered *tabua* to all the villages that Baker passed through. The action of the Naitasiri chief's *tabua* "following" Baker's meant that the missionary's offering and guarantee of safe passage became obsolete. In the

Figure 1. Missionary display case at the Fiji Museum. Photograph by Katrina Talei Igglesden, 2013.

Figure 2. Church built as memorial to Baker and his men on the actual site of Baker's residence. Baker's bones and shoe remains were kept here until they were presented to the Museum in 1973. Photograph courtesy of the Fiji Museum.

manner of indigenous Fijian custom, the first *tabua* was "struck" down, an act known as *dirika*. In most villages, the second *tabua* was refused and Baker's *tabua* remained valid, except in Nagagadelavatu, where the chief Nawawabalavu accepted Naitasiri's *tabua* (Tomlinson 2012, 222). The main purpose of offering a second *tabua* was "to ensure that Ratu Cakobau's religion would be stopped and not proceed further" (Clunie 2013, personal communication). Ratu Seru Cakobau, who held the position of Vunivalu (war-chief) of Bau, had converted to Christianity in 1854 and was baptised in 1857 by the Wesleyan Methodist missionary Reverend Joseph Waterhouse. He was strategically spreading his influence.

Not only did the Naitasiri *tabua* materialise a refusal to accept Christianity, but the very acceptance of the second whale's tooth ultimately led to the killing of Reverend Baker. This act must have come as a surprise to Baker's party as the chief Nawawabalavu had earlier allowed them to enter the village and hold a church service. Having warned Baker that he might be in danger, he then led the party out of the village himself and into an ambush. A group of Nagagadelavatu men with faces blackened for war attacked Baker's group, one warrior felling Baker with an axe named *Tevedriu* (Wesley 2008). Minister Setareki Seileka and six students were also killed alongside Baker, and all eight bodies were cleaned and prepared for the earth oven (*lovo*). An old lady who saw Baker's body lamented upon seeing it and scolded Nawawabalavu and his men for the murder of God's anointed (Wood 1978, 162).

When considering the now infamous killing of Baker and his colleagues, it is important to address the mystification surrounding his death. One descendant of Nawawabalavu claims that Baker met his fate because he dared to touch his ancestor's head when reclaiming his comb from him (Thomson 1894; Derrick 1946, 165), and this explains why Baker was killed while under the chief's protection. He insists, however, that Nawawabalavu decided to overlook the offence but his *bati*, the warrior clan who serve a chief, were determined that Baker should be reprimanded for his wrongdoing (Wesley 2008). According to indigenous Fijian beliefs, the head is the most important and sacred part of the body; it is the seat of a person's glory, power and knowledge. One must never touch a person's hair or head without asking permission, or stand above a person of high status (Gravelle 1979, 106). If it proves unavoidable, then the inferior must stoop low and walk past saying "*tulou*" (pardon). If the myth of Reverend Baker accurately records that he touched Nawawabalavu's hair, then this would incur severe consequences for the missionary. As an action punishable by death, it is feasible to see how this explanation has been perpetuated over the last century. However, at the time of his death, Baker was not a newcomer to Fijian culture. He had already spent eight years in Fiji, spoke the language well and knew the customs of the land. He therefore would have known that touching a chief's head would cause trouble and mistrust to ensue. In order to succeed in the conversion of "heathen" Fijians, Baker would have been very careful in his relations with chiefs, those who had the capability to be his closest and most valuable allies. Mass conversions to Christianity often occurred in the wake of powerful chiefs converting, as was most notably evidenced in 1854 by Ratu Seru Cakobau *lotu*-ing, i.e. converting to Christianity (*lotu*); this single event virtually assured the success of the Methodist Mission in Fiji (Toren 1995, 166).

Boyd (1919, cited in Derrick 1946, 165) has asserted that it was Christianity that was being condemned in the murder of Baker, not the man himself. He states that if Baker had not been a missionary, he and his party would have been warmly welcomed into the interior of Viti Levu. However, Baker's close association with Ratu Seru Cakobau as the priest of "his religion" almost guaranteed that he would face hostility from the mountain people, who refused to become subservient to Cakobau's powerful Bau chiefdom and its allies. Baker had a premonition of his fate whilst stationed in Bua, during an incident when his canoe came across a band of men from the neighbouring province of Macuata. These men had just killed their *bete*, a priest from the Old Religion, and were hurling abuse at Baker and his crew. At Rev. Baker's insistence, the Christian group remained silent in the face of the unfolding provocations. Baker later wrote in his journal, "I thought Fiji had not yet stained its shores with a missionary's blood…Am I to be the first?"

(Wood 1978, 159). Coastal people warned Baker about the hill tribes of Viti Levu's interior, as many were hostile to Christianity and had an aversion to anything exported inland from the coast. Baker chose not to heed these warnings, as the traveller and collector George Boyne noted in his papers. He reported that Baker had been working on a chart of the island and was keen to go inland to see the area for himself in order to accurately finish the map. Even after he was warned of the dangers, he replied that he had eight years of experience and could handle whatever he encountered.[33]

Insulting to all Fijians, another narrative that has circulated is that the shoe soles on display in the Fiji Museum are the only remains left uneaten because the villagers of Nagagadelavatu could not chew the soles. Fijians are sensitive about Fiji's cannibal past, and this statement continues to be vehemently refuted by the chief's descendants. In actual fact, the shoe soles are the remains of Reverend Baker's spare boots, which were being carried by one of the two survivors of the massacre at the time of the attack. He flung them away in his hurry to escape. Many years later, following a bush fire, these remnants were found in a reed clump at the site of the massacre, Nagagadelavatu, Navosa. Today, Nagagadelavatu village no longer exists. It was demolished soon after Baker's death and the site has since been left untouched. The entire population of the village moved to a new site called Nabutautau. The Reverend Arthur J. Small visited the demolished village site in 1885, and found the earth oven (*lovo*) that Baker and his party were baked in still intact, having never been used again after that day in 1867. While visiting, Reverend Small found a small bone wedged in the fork of a tree, which he believed to be part of Baker's remains and took back to Davuilevu, where Baker, his wife and three daughters were stationed at the time of his death. A church named Baker Memorial Hall opened on 14 October 1913 and now stands on the site of their residence, in memory of Baker and the other men who died.

After Baker's death, the people of Nagagadelavatu village developed a belief that they were under a curse because they had dared to touch one of God's anointed. In order to counteract this curse, the people of Navosa Province, on behalf of themselves and the village of Nagagadelavatu, presented a *tabua* whale's tooth to the Wesleyan church as a formal request for forgiveness (*soro*). Later, in 1903, the Navuso (Naitasiri) chief presented another *tabua* to ask for forgiveness for his ancestor's part in the killing. This *tabua* is now on display in the Fiji Museum and was given as an offering of humility and repentance (Gravelle 1979, 106). In 1985, Lynne Flaherty, one of Baker's descendants, visited Nabutautau and presented the villagers with another *tabua*. With her offering she was asking the villagers and their ancestors to forgive her own ancestor for any wrongdoings on his part when he was in Fiji. Almost twenty years later, in November 2003, ten Australian descendants of Reverend Baker travelled to Nabutautau village where the descendants of Nawawabalavu and the people of Nagagadelavatu asked for forgiveness for the missionary's death 136 years earlier. The elaborate reconciliation

33 Boyne, G. 1865-9. *The Boyne Papers. 1. An Account of the Fiji Islands together with Contemporary Accounts of Certain Incidents*, 5-6. Unpublished Manuscript, Fiji Museum Manuscripts Collection.

ceremony featured a re-enactment of the events leading up to Baker's death, and included the presentation of traditional valuables to Baker's family, such as finely woven mats, a dozen *tabua* and a slaughtered cow. This ceremony was not only attended by the descendants of Baker and the villagers, but also the great grandson of the Naitasiri chief who had "struck down" Baker's *tabua* and ordered his death, alongside Fiji's then Prime Minister Laisenia Qarase. A ceremony such as this had never previously occurred in Fiji, and many Fijians from the interior of Viti Levu travelled to witness the event. Both a joyous and sad occasion, one of Baker's descendants made a speech which thanked the villagers for their humility and kindness towards them, and explained that, although Baker's death was a tragedy in their family, there was no hatred borne toward the community where the crime had been committed. At the end of the six-hour ceremony, the descendants of Nawawabalavu felt that their curse had been lifted (Squires 2003).

It is these events – the killing of a missionary, and its consequences for the relatives of all parties involved – that are indirectly displayed in the Fiji Museum case containing the remains of Baker's shoes. His boots share the gallery space with another display case focusing on pre-Christian practices and containing objects used in the Old Religion, such as a walking stick, a necklace and *yaqona* vessels to summon the old gods of Fiji. The juxtaposition of both cases is an apt representation of what has happened in Fiji's history, with Christianity and the gods of the Old Religion vying for the attention of its people. Since the late nineteenth century, Christianity has become widespread in Fiji. Methodism, other Protestant denominations and Catholicism have the largest number of supporters, followed by non-Christian religions including Hinduism, Islam and Sikhism. While pre-Christian gods such as *Degei* are no longer worshipped openly, they are still sometimes acknowledged and placated to ensure good fortune and well-being (Toren 1995, 166). Such gods are considered to live under the Christian God, but continue to impress historic relationships on their descendants through their connection to the land and their past role in the cycles of production, consumption, exchange and sacrifice. The most problematic part of this legacy for Christian Fiji, however, is the notion that such gods can still be empowered by those who offer them sacrifices to unleash their malign powers (Toren 1995, 167). As many objects in the Fiji Museum are connected to pre-Christian practices, how have the Fiji Museum and its collections been viewed by Christian Fijians?

The majority of Christian Fijians believe that all objects in the museum's collection contain spirits which could adversely affect their health and fortunes. Even if artefacts are unrelated to the Old Religion, there is a general consensus that they are malicious or demonic things because of their close physical proximity to things from pre-Christian times. Because the museum has a reputation of housing malevolent objects, there have been cases where certain types of objects, mostly *tabua*, have been donated to the museum because the donor believed the object to be cursed and causing sickness within their family, and therefore could no longer have the object in the house. Conversely, a belief in curses also leads the museum to receive requests for the return of such objects: in 1997/1998, the community of one village made an appeal for a *wasekaseka* necklace of split whale teeth to be returned. According to the villagers, the necklace was so powerful and malevolent that it was believed to be causing deaths in the village, even though it was housed far away in the museum. In a desperate attempt to have the object returned to them and prevent future deaths, they threatened to burn the museum down if they were not given the necklace back. Between 2003 and 2005, many breakaway Protestant churches called for their members to bring forward so-called problematic heirlooms such as *tabua* and clubs and burn them in order to prove, renew and strengthen their Christian belief and commitment. In response to these burnings, the museum issued an advertisement in local newspapers requesting that anyone interested in the safe disposal of their heirlooms should consider the museum as an option. By this means, one particular large *tabua* came into the Museum's care, and has since been placed in the Museum's secure storage area.

The spiritual aspect of the collection is one that Fiji Museum staff members have encountered on a multitude of levels and it is one that can contradict with some staff members' dual role as safeguarders of cultural heritage and devout Christians. Help from Christian church members has been sought on numerous occasions to pray for the protection, well-being and good fortune of the institution, its staff and collections.

1. Exterior of the Church, with congregation assembling.
2. Reading the Request of the Trustees for Consecration.
3. The Bishop of Melanesia (the Right Rev. J. R. Selwyn).
4, 5, and 6. Native Students of Melanesian Church Mission.

CONSECRATION OF THE BISHOP PATTESON MEMORIAL CHURCH (ST. BARNABAS), NORFOLK ISLAND.—SEE PRECEDING PAGE.

Bishop Patteson relics, Solomon Islands

Ben Wate

Fairy tales in Europe and *Kastom Story* in Melanesia often end similarly with "and they lived happily ever after". This short phrase suggests positive outcomes after overcoming misfortune and bad experiences. The story of the Melanesian Mission and the martyrdom of Bishop John Coleridge Patteson is a popular narrative in Anglican Melanesia (Solomon Islands, Vanuatu and the French Territory of New Caledonia). This intangible 'relic' survives in the Pacific to be told to children and is used to bring to mind an historical narrative about human value and dignity and the transformation of a community and culture to Christianity. Told in homes, Sunday Schools and Church schools, it has become part of the Melanesian Mission history courses taught in the Church Theological institutions, including the Bishop Patteson Theological College, Kohimarama in Solomon Islands.

Patteson was killed on the beach at Nukapu on 20 September 1871, out of revenge for the recent forcible removal of five men by labour recruiters. In the aftermath of his death, his body was wrapped in a mat and five knotted palm fronds were placed over the club and arrow wounds on his body. These palm fronds were said to mark his murder as revenge for the five kidnapped men. But over time the palm fronds have become the 'the marks of the Lord Jesus' placed on the wounds his body sustained. The mat, knotted palm fronds and several personal possessions, such as his Bible are today enshrined in the Cathedral in Honiara. The narration of the brutal death episode of Bishop Patteson at Nukapu is no longer the story of an ordinary English Missionary Bishop whose fatal journey ended on Nukapu. It is instead the story of a 'grandfather' who brought Anglican Christianity to Melanesia. Patteson has thus been adopted into the general order of kinship in Melanesia and is celebrated and acknowledged through churches, enshrined relics, missionary archives, oral histories and names – many islanders have adopted and use Patteson as a name for their children. In this way the narrative of his death has new theological meaning in the Pacific, beyond the brutality surrounding his death. His advice, words and deeds, his books, manuscripts, photographs, portraits and furniture are relics of power which add physical form to this narrative. In Britain,

Figure 1. Congregation of the Bishop Patteson Memorial Church, Norfolk Island, the first of several churches dedicated to the memory of Bishop Patteson and used to house and display relics associated with his death. From *Illustrated London News*, 12 March 1881, 252.

where Patteson's death caused public outrage and led to government intervention into the recruiting trade, Patteson remains largely unknown today. In Melanesia the resonance of that moment is not historic, but rather present in the buildings, relics and lives of Melanesian Anglicans today.

Commemoration of Patteson and his deeds was immediate. After his death, a memorial cross was erected at Nukapu, with the following inscription:

> *In Memory of John Coleridge Patteson, Missionary Bishop, whose life was taken by men for whom he would gladly have given it. September 20, 1871.*

Less than a decade later, in 1880, the Bishop Patteson Memorial Church (St Barnabas) on Norfolk Island was consecrated. By 1928 the Patteson relics were enshrined in the newly built St Luke's cathedral in Siota on Nggela Island. In the late 1940s, All Saints Cathedral became the temporary cathedral in Honiara soon after it became the administrative capital of the islands. Finally, this was replaced by the St Barnabas' Cathedral, which opened in 1968. Each venue housed the relics associated with Patteson and hosted the annual commemorative Lesser Festival on 20 September, the anniversary of his death. Part of the worldwide Anglican calendar, Lesser Festivals acknowledge an individual but it is not compulsory to mark them with an event. In Solomon Islands, the festival is observed and Patteson is commemorated for his saintly life and as a martyr. The church community mark the day with feasting and island dancing and the day's sermon guides the celebration. The sermon emphasizes the significant contribution of Bishop Patteson to the Melanesians in his role as foreign missionary. It acknowledges the challenge he undertook to travel far from home and become resident amongst the Melanesian islanders. For Melanesian Anglicans this annual day of celebration and commemoration moves 'Bishop Patteson' – as he is called in Melanesia – beyond the individual into the social and cultural imagination of the Anglican Melanesian World.

'Bishop Patteson' was not an ordinary bishop in the episcopal ranking in the Anglican Church of New Zealand. He was assigned missionary responsibility for Melanesians and undertook to ensure they received the same respect and teachings that Anglicans of European and Maori descent received. He believed that the Melanesian boys and girls who were brought to New Zealand should be allowed to attend the same mission school that both Europeans and Maori attended, but that special consideration should be made to understand the impact of the cold climate and weather conditions of New Zealand. In 1859, a Melanesian School was established at Kohimarama on the southern shore of Auckland harbour, having been moved from St. Johns College on the hilltop. Funded by Bishop Patteson's cousin Charlotte Yonge (Hilliard 1978: 30), it provided a warmer climate and focused syllabus for the Melanesian students.

His views stood out from his contemporaries and even his superior, Bishop George Augustus Selwyn, who founded the Melanesian Mission in 1849. As an accomplished linguist, having learnt 23 Melanesian languages, Patteson was troubled over Selwyn's strategy to make the English language the *lingua franca* in the fragmented islands of Melanesia. Patteson doubted the efficacy of this policy given the diverse and numerous languages spoken in the islands. At the Melanesian school of Kohimarama, Banks Islanders were dominant and Mota became popular as other islanders found it easier to speak. For Patteson this furthered his approach that Melanesians should meet Christ in their homes not on foreign soil. It also meant that Melanesian cultures and languages should be used in Christian instruction and worship, making it more compatible and integrated with Melanesian religious beliefs and ways of life. In 1867, Patteson declared Mota as *lingua franca* for the Melanesian Mission. In the same year, he relocated the Melanesian school at Kohimarama to Norfolk Island, even though Bishop Selwyn believed that New Zealand, as the headquarters of the Melanesian Mission, should host the schools and teach in English.

Patteson believed that Melanesians did not need to "denationalize" from Melanesian culture and absorb English culture when becoming Christian. He maintained that being sympathetic to Melanesian culture does not imply a change to the fundamental principles of Christianity. He hoped to see a Christianity that was faithful to the scripture, sound in rationality and faithful to the fundamental teachings of Christianity. Patteson's long and steadfast concern for Melanesians has earned him respect in Melanesia and led to him occupying a larger space in the Melanesian world of social, political and religious life. His brutal death at Nukapu, at the hands of those he was presented to as a friend, challenged the local people's view of white men. Melanesians later came to see that Patteson was a scapegoat for the attempt to force islanders into participating in a form of slavery for cheap wages. The fact that Patteson was tricked through other white men's sheer selfish attitude for money challenged the Melanesian view of white people as gods. His death became an example of the fallible nature of the whites.

The fact that Patteson's skin colour might have been white does not overshadow his spirit of sympathy for Melanesians. The islanders knew his name as Bishop Patteson, but his social life with Melanesians was space-less because he created no space or gap as he related to them through sharing of food, spoke their languages, prayed and taught them the love and forgiveness of God. These facts have enabled Patteson to become a Melanesian culture hero, embedded within the world of Melanesia. He is a Melanesian grandfather, in a new kinship system reconstructed by the Melanesian Mission for the Melanesians. This intangible heritage reaches beyond those tangible relics enshrined in the physical space of the cathedral into the stories and lives of Anglican Melanesians today.

"African Church", Botswana

Paul Lane

On a rocky terrace near the foot of the main northern escarpment of the Tswapong Hills stand the remains of a large brick-built church, designed to hold a thousand worshippers (Figure 1). Now a gazetted national monument in Botswana, the church was constructed between 1891 and 1893 and largely paid for by Khama III, then ruler of the Bangwato people. In 1889, Khama had ordered the relocation of his capital from Shoshong, sixty miles away, to the new town of Phalatswe. One European participant estimated that this involved the relocation of 15,000-20,000 inhabitants. Phalatswe was laid out, buildings erected and the previous capital Shoshong vacated over just a few weeks between July and September of that year. While such large-scale moves appear to have been a fairly regular event in Tswana history, what is more unusual about this move is that Khama was a Christian. He expected missionaries from the London Missionary Society to relocate with the town, and while he financed the relocation of the mission and the building of a new church, surrounding events suggest that Khama's relationships with missionaries were far from straightforward.

The London Missionary Society (LMS) had been particularly instrumental in the introduction of Christianity to a number of different north-western Tswana groups in what is now eastern Botswana. Along with David Livingstone, who worked among the Bakwena from 1847–1852 while based at Kolobeng, LMS missionaries were also active among their more powerful neighbours to the north – the Bangwato. Although Livingstone visited the Bangwato in 1842, it was not until 1859 that the first converts were baptised – by a Lutheran missionary from the Hermannsburg Mission, Christoph Schulenburg. Among Schulenburg's early converts was Boikanyo Khama (later Khama III), who was baptised in 1862. Khama was the son of the then Bangwato ruler *Kgosi* Sekgoma I, and became a fervent convert to Christianity. On becoming the Bangwato ruler in 1875, after ousting his father, he introduced a number of social and ideological reforms among his people, including the prohibition of initiation ceremonies, polygamy and bridewealth payments, and the banning of European liquor and traditional beer. He also encouraged his subjects to attend church and observe the Sabbath. To this end, throughout his rule Khama III facilitated the presence of LMS missionaries,

Figure 1. View of the northeast end of the African Church at Phalatswe in 2013, looking northwest. Photograph by Ceri Ashley.

who succeeded the Hermannsburg organisation following their withdrawal from Shoshong in 1863.

The first LMS missionaries to arrive, from their base at Kuruman, were the Reverends John MacKenzie and Roger Price, who began work in Shoshong in 1862. Between them, Price (who left Shoshong in 1865 for the Bakwena capital at Ntsweng) and MacKenzie (who returned to Kuruman in 1876) built up a busy mission station which eventually consisted of a stone-walled thatched church and several rectangular stone-walled houses for the missionaries (MacKenzie 1871), the remains of which can still be seen today (as can Livingstone's house at Kolobeng). MacKenzie was joined in August 1871 by the Reverend James Hepburn and his family, who remained at Shoshong until it was abandoned in 1889. The precise reasons for this move are unclear. Hepburn mentions the shortage of water as the principle cause, and several European visitors to Shoshong in the late 1880s described the town as "filthy" and disease-infested. Other factors, including concerns over threats to the security of the Ngwato polity from Boer and Matabele expansion, also appear to have shaped Khama's decision (Parsons 1973).

Building a Mission

When Hepburn and his family first arrived at Phalatswe, they lived in their wagon and a few roughly constructed "huts", which formed Hepburn's main base as he set about the process of re-establishing the material presence of the mission among the Bangwato. A visitor to the town in 1890 described the site of the mission as being "a mile from the town, on one side of a large hill, clothed thickly with cactus and other trees ... From the house door you look over the city – or rather the group of five villages which together form this well-designed Palapye" (*Cape Argus* 23 October 1890, cited in Hepburn 1970, 316). Behind the "house" was a "beautiful gorge" with "the most romantic waterfall, overhung with ferns" at one end, "amongst other trees in the wildest luxuriance, the candelabra-like cactus, the flowering aloe, the elephant tree, the mimosa, the fig tree, the wild cotton creeper, and a large variety of curious and lovely flowers" (*ibid.*, 316-7). While its location may well have pleased Hepburn, it is unlikely that he had much say in the initial choice as it was Khama who arranged for the construction of the "huts" used by Hepburn and his family as their new home (Hepburn 1970, 310). Other evidence also suggests that Khama clearly intended the mission to be physically separated from the main town (Reid *et al.* 1997).

Subsequently, "a more commodious 'mud and pole shanty' – roofed with corrugated iron – was erected" for the mission (Hepburn 1970, 310). This was a long, narrow, rectangular structure built of puddled mud with roughly hewn timber uprights, and simple, calico-covered apertures for windows (*ibid.*, 337-8). Initially, Hepburn was content to suffer the privations of this new accommodation, which was in marked contrast to the more substantial, stone-built house he and his family had left behind at Shoshong, arguing, "A church first, a house for myself and my family afterwards" (*ibid.*, 338). By January 1891, however, the rains had already begun to take their toll, prompting Hepburn to complain to his LMS superiors at Kuruman that his house was "very visibly going to pieces. The rain comes through its walls and roof ... [destroying] papers and books ... food and clothing" (*ibid.*, 342-3). Hepburn's growing sense of frustration with the LMS authorities at Kuruman was not helped by the continuing postponement of the start of work on the construction of a new church. His frustration over the delays is evident in a letter he wrote in January 1891 to his superiors at Kuruman:

> *But to go on yet again, on through another year into the next without the shelter of a House of God for the people, is an outlook too hopeless. I cannot endure it, and I am persuaded it would carry with it most serious injury to the Mission.* (Hepburn 1970, 343)

Work did begin on the church in 1891, but progress was slow due to Hepburn's deteriorating relationship with Khama III. In the end, Hepburn left Phalatswe towards the end of the year under something of a cloud, having fallen out with Khama. This was ostensibly over the use of non-Christian labour to assist with the building of the African Church, but was also connected with disagreements with his fellow missionaries and the LMS as a whole, from which Hepburn was trying to break away in order to establish his own independent mission. However, there was also a deeper problem regarding the question of ownership of the land on which the mission and African Church were built. Under Tswana law, all land belongs to the *kgosi* (king/chief, plural *dikgosi*), and Khama's understanding was that the land had been loaned to the mission. Hepburn, however, wanted recognition that the land was owned by the LMS, since this would give the Church legal authority over the space occupied by the mission. Khama (cited in Mgadla 1986, 143) was sufficiently displeased to write to Hepburn's superiors at Kuruman informing them that he did "not wish Hepburn to return to teach" in the town, and requested that another missionary be sent to replace him.

In due course, in 1893, the Reverend W. D. Willoughby took up the appointment, and remained at Phalatswe until Khama moved his capital once again, in 1902, to Serowe, where it has remained. Willoughby's relationship with Khama seems to have been an easier one, and he was instrumental in arranging Khama's trip to England in 1895, along with Chiefs Sebele and Bathoen (the *dikgosi* of the Bakwena and Bangwaketse, respectively), to meet Queen Victoria (Parsons 1998). However, the dispute over ownership of the land on which the mission was located re-emerged several more times, and was never fully resolved. Khama, in other words, shared many of the concerns of other Tswana *dikgosi* about the dangers of relinquishing authority over even part of their territory to the missionaries.

The Phalatswe Mission, 1889–1902

Ultimately, the LMS mission at Phalatswe had five components: the mission station, with houses for the missionaries who later included a number of unmarried women employed as schoolteachers; the "Native" or "African" church; an "English" church where services were conducted in English for the resident European

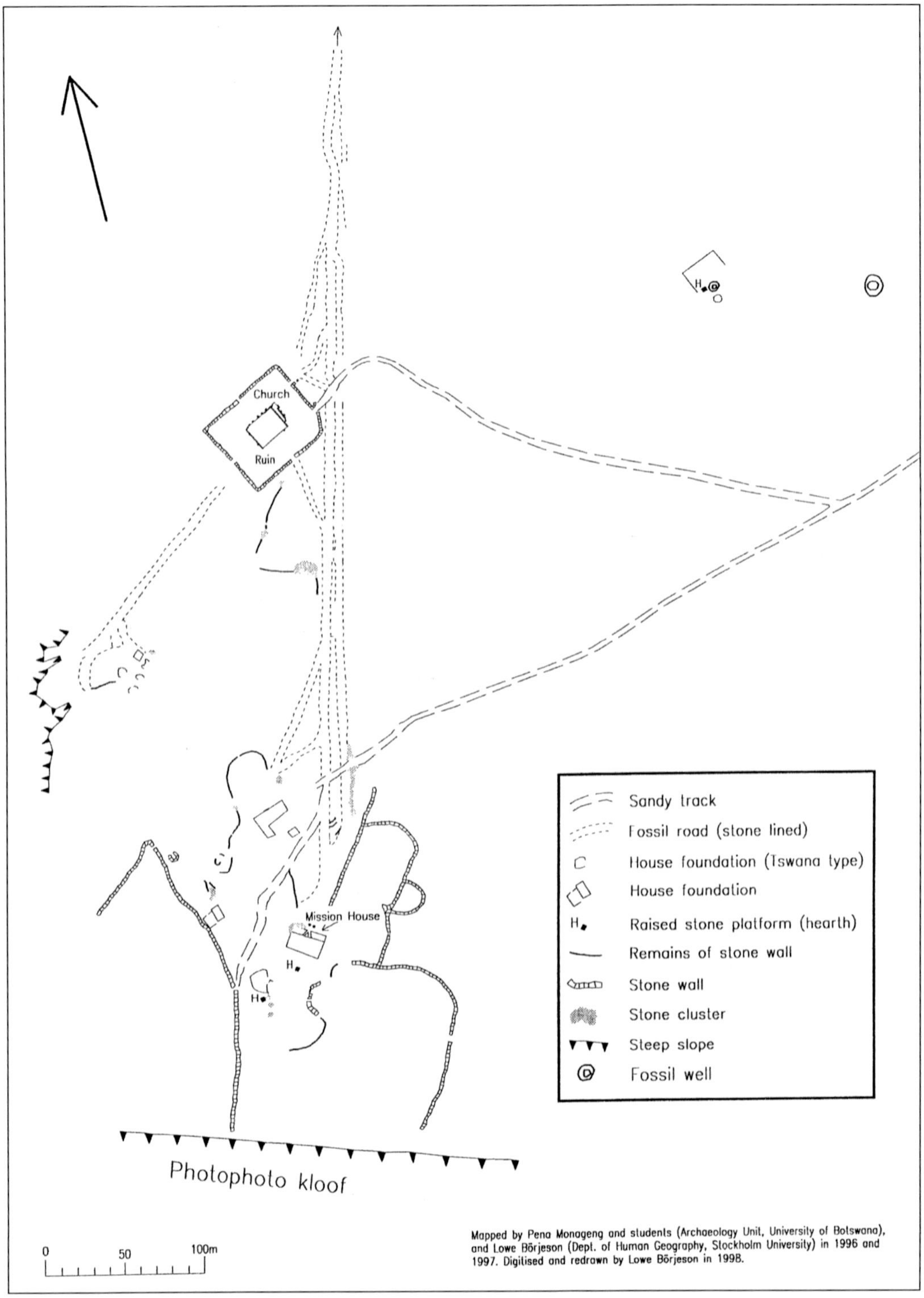

Figure 2. Plan of the surviving remains around the LMS mission site at Phalatswe; the African church is located in the top left portion of the image. Source: plan prepared by Lowe Börjeson, based on original survey data compiled by Pena Monageng, Lowe Börjeson and University of Botswana archaeology students in 1995 & 1996.

population (mostly traders and those involved in the colonial administration of the Bechuanaland Protectorate established in 1885); a "central school" run by the mission and linked to other "schools" distributed throughout the settlement; and a Christian cemetery or cemeteries. The remains of many of these elements and significant portions of the town itself survive as archaeological traces in the landscape today (Börjeson and Lane 1996). By far the most substantial and dramatic of these are the remains of the African church (Figure 2).

When the church was completed in 1893, the total cost of the building work was recorded as having been over £4,000 (excluding the bell-tower), most of which was provided by Khama III with additional contributions from his subjects. In plan, the building was of a fairly standard basilica type, measuring c. 24 x 15m, the main body consisting of a rectangular nave on a raised stone foundation, flanked by aisles on either side. Each of the aisles had five arched lancet windows along its length, interspersed by brick buttresses. The walls, which reached c. 15m high at the two ends, were built of roughly fired red brick, which surviving traces suggest were mud-plastered on the inside. The building was aligned southwest-northeast with a narrow portico at the northeast end of the building, in which an arched doorway was set. This served as the primary entrance. The altar was situated at the southwestern end, on a raised dais approached by three steps, with a small doorway on the southern side.

Although the church was intended to accommodate a thousand worshippers, records suggest that the size of the congregation was rarely above three hundred. A photograph taken by Willoughby of the interior shows a floor of beaten earth, a prayer desk and a number of folding wooden chairs and stools for the congregation clustered around the altar dais, on which three more formal chairs are standing, but little else in the way of internal furnishing or decoration. Music was provided by an American organ donated in 1893 by a European trader, Samuel Blackbeard, who had also moved to Phalatswe from Shoshong. Aside from the windows along the aisles, the interior was lit by a row of clerestory windows above each side of the nave, three lancet windows at the north-eastern end above the portico and a rose window at the altar end (Figure 3). Corrugated iron sheets were used for all the roofing.

An 1897 photograph shows a rectangular bell-tower to the right (north) of the entrance. This was only completed that same year, and initially housed a two-and-a-half ton bell donated by Khama. However, it quickly transpired that it could not be heard in the town on the plain below, and the bell was moved to the "English" church from where it appears to have been audible. Today, only the ends of the building and parts of the portico and bell-tower walls are still standing, although the floor and foundations are still visible (see Figure 1).

The African Church was approached from three separate directions by different roads, constructed at various times during the occupation of Phalatswe (see Figure 2). Two of these roads – the one from the LMS mission station slightly further up the hillside to the west, and the one running roughly north-south upslope from the plains below, where the main town was situated – are marked by lines of large stones placed on either side of the track. The road that runs west-east

Figure 3. Detailed view of the interior wall and rose window of the southwest end of the African church in 2013; note recent restoration work on the upper part of the rose window.
Photograph by Ceri Ashley.

between the church and the area where most Europeans, including the resident commissioner, had their dwellings was probably among the first to be built. This track now provides the main access route to the site of the church. Since Hepburn and his family based themselves in the area adjacent to the Photophoto gorge after their arrival from Shoshong, some of the smaller paths that radiate out from the

African Church probably date from this initial phase of building work. The road linking the church with the core of the settlement was the last to be constructed, in 1894, when the stone wall around the church was also added. It became known as "the New Road".

Conclusion

Aside from its importance as a gazetted National Monument, the African Church at Phalatswe is significant for at least two, rather contradictory reasons. First, at the time of its construction the church was the largest and most substantial example of its type in the Bechuanaland Protectorate. As such, it may well have become a key symbol of the commitment felt towards Christianity by the Bangwato at that time. Second, the building of the church, or some other actions connected with it, also appears to have been a contributory cause of the rift between Khama III and the LMS missionary Reverend James Hepburn, which contributed to Hepburn's effective expulsion despite his earlier cordial relationships with Khama. The building of the church was always a social and political act, and as such the material fabric of the building intended as a "House of God" inevitably became a contested space, entangled in competing discourses concerning both old and new imaginings of the spiritual and cultural landscape of the Bangwato and Christianity. Its subsequent abandonment and neglect provides an unequivocal signal as to whose power – that of Khama or that of the LMS missionaries – ultimately triumphed.

JOHN WIL

Ship's bell, United Kingdom

Chris Wingfield

Encountering this bell, impressed in large black letters with the words "JOHN WILLIAMS", in the far corner of a modern office block basement in Westminster, London, in August 2010 was something of a surprise. Although it sat clapperless on the floor, its large white painted metal bracket suggested that it had once been fixed to a wall in a way that allowed it to swing from side to side. On closer inspection, its upper surface appeared to be covered in small drops of white paint, while its underside showed the characteristic white tidemarks of dried salt water. These different marks, on the upper and lower surfaces of the bell, are suggestive of the bell's century-long biography linking London to the islands of the Pacific.

The office in question belonged to the Council for World Mission (CWM), the successor organization to the London Missionary Society (LMS), who had moved here from their previous headquarters at nearby Livingstone House in 1997. An accumulation of material associated with the long history of the London Missionary Society (established in 1795) had moved with the organization, but was largely stored with the bell in the basement, where its presence did not disrupt the apparent efficient modernity of the workspaces above ground. In working my way through this assemblage of material, I soon came upon the bell's missing clapper, attached to a short length of rope, and a small plastic display label that declared:

> BELL OF THE
> S.S. JOHN WILLIAMS
> 1894 – 1930

The SS *John Williams* was a steamship that was built for the LMS in 1893, and in technical language was a "clipper-bowed barquentine of 663 tons with auxiliary steam powered propulsion" (Powerhouse Museum, n.d.). In laymen's language, although she had a steam-powered propeller, she could also be sailed with the three magnificent sails that rose from the deck. The ship was built and launched on the Clyde in Scotland, but mainly spent her working life carrying people, goods, and letters between Sydney in Australia and mission stations in New Guinea and on Pacific Islands. The ship completed an annual round of

Figure 1. Bell of the SS John Williams 1894–1930. Discovered in a basement in London, now at the National Maritime Museum (ZBA5548). Photograph by Chris Wingfield.

30,000 miles of sailing until 1930, when she was sold to Chinese buyers, having completed an estimated million miles in the service of the LMS (Northcott 1945, 54). The SS *John Williams* was actually the fourth in a line of LMS ships to bear this name until the decommissioning of *John Williams VII* in 1968, two years after the London Missionary Society had ceased to be known by that name. The original John Williams was not a ship but a missionary, and was probably the most famous nineteenth-century missionary until his fame was eclipsed by that of David Livingstone.

John Williams (1796–1839) was sent by the London Missionary Society to the Pacific in 1817, but returned to Britain in 1834 to supervise the printing of a Rarotongan New Testament. While in Britain, Williams also published a famous account of his work, *Narratives of Missionary Enterprises in the South Sea Islands* (Williams 1837), and engaged in a hectic round of speaking engagements, widespread lobbying and fundraising.

Williams was determined that the London Missionary Society needed its own ship in order to work more effectively in the Pacific, and in the space of four years managed to raise the money to commission one, the *Camden*, in which he returned to the Pacific in 1837. Unfortunately for Williams, he was killed in what is now Vanuatu in November 1839, but this had the effect of enhancing his reputation considerably, and he went from being referred to as the "Apostle of Polynesia" to the "Martyr of Erromango" (see Mayer, this volume).

The Directors of the London Missionary Society were not slow to appreciate the general interest in John Williams' death and the widely felt need to commemorate his life. In 1843, a fundraising campaign was launched among children that raised £6,000, and a ship that bore his name was launched in 1844. It was officially based in London and returned every five years laden with goods from the Pacific, at which point maintenance was again paid for by money raised by child supporters. *John Williams I* was wrecked in May 1864 at Pukapuka Island and replaced by *John Williams II*, also wrecked shortly afterwards at Niue in June 1867. *John Williams III* was the first LMS ship to be based in Sydney rather than London, and survived until 1895, when she was sold and replaced by the SS *John Williams*.

The particular attraction of these ships for young people seems to have been widely recognised, with one LMS writer (Northcott 1945, 55) suggesting in 1945 that:

> *For three generations of children and schools and churches in Britain and Australia and New Zealand the ship has provided the romantic entrance to the missionary enterprise. She has opened the gate of wonder and surprise and created a great volume of love and support for the L.M.S. How many people date their own care and concern to "collecting for the ship"?*

These ships featured regularly in promotional literature, as imagery on missionary collecting boxes, and models and images of the *John Williams* ships were also displayed in the London Missionary Society Museum (1814-1910) alongside objects collected in different parts of the world. At a children's celebration of the centenary of the LMS in 1895, a model of the SS *John Williams* was launched into the fountain of the Crystal Palace. In 1945, it was estimated that over the previous century, £560,000 had been raised by children to support the maintenance and building of these ships (Northcott 1945, 55).

Given that many children appear to have grown up with a particular emotional attachment to the *John Williams*, it is perhaps no wonder that relics of LMS ships, such as the bell from the SS *John Williams*, were preserved at the LMS headquarters in London to be visited, seen and touched by supporters, young and old.

While the bell can be regarded as a relic of a particular ship, in another sense, the *John Williams* ships appear to have been regarded as something of a relic of the missionary whose name they bore. *South Seas Sailor: The Story of John Williams and His Ships,* a book published for children in 1965, ends with the suggestion that "John Williams sails on in his ships and the message of Christ is the same as he preached a hundred and fifty years ago" (Northcott 1965, 95).

Following its installation at Livingstone House in London, this bell may have served as a reminder of such sentiments, but it also appears to have served another purpose. In 2010, a retired missionary recalled that prayer times at LMS headquarters had been marked by ringing this bell. In 2013 the bell began a new life when it was acquired by the National Maritime Museum in Greenwich (accession number ZBA5548), along with the majority of the other material from the CWM basement. While it will no doubt enrich the NMM collections, and enable new stories about Britain's maritime past to be told, it seems likely that it will again be regarded as less of a relic, and more of an artefact.

A green dress, Vanuatu

Carol E. Mayer

This green dress (Figure 1) was made in 2009 by Jocelyn Natgo, a descendant of the Natgo clan, which originates in Erromango, one of the islands that comprise the Republic of Vanuatu. Jocelyn made this dress in Port Vila, the capital of Vanuatu, where many of her clan members now make their home. It is an *aelan dres* (island dress) of the style typically worn by women in the central and southern regions of Erromango, introduced by Presbyterian missionaries who viewed modesty as a primary virtue and expected converts to Christianity to clothe themselves accordingly. The result, with some stylistic variations, is a very loose fitting dress with a high neckline, short sleeves, and floating flaps, often referred to as wings, attached to the skirt. However, although the island dress is still worn to church, it is now mostly viewed as a national symbol to be worn for important occasions and also as an expression of people's sense of home and belonging (Bolton 2007, 180). This dress was made in 2009 for an important occasion. It was made specifically for me, a curator at the Museum of Anthropology (MOA), University of British Columbia, Vancouver, Canada, and was donated to the collection in 2014. Its acceptance into the collection was based not so much on its physical or cultural attributes but on its role as tangible evidence of an event of national importance.

The incentive for this event came in 2006 when I received a phone call from Daisy Williams, the wife of Michael Williams, a descendant of the Reverend John Williams (1796–1839), a missionary of the London Missionary Society (LMS) who was killed on the shores of Erromango in 1839. In 1886, Sidney Williams, the grandson of John Williams, moved from England to settle in British Columbia where he married a First Nations woman, Agnes Amelia Shepherd – granddaughter of Chief Joseph of the Lil'wat Nation. Sidney Williams brought with him some of the artefacts collected by his grandfather during his time in the Pacific. These were passed down in the family until the decision was made for them to be placed in a Canadian museum that held a Pacific Islands collection. There were five artefacts: a New Caledonian bird's head club, an Austral Islands whisk, a Fijian/Tongan club, a Tongan fishhook and a Māori flute. When they were brought to the museum, they were viewed as important additions to the South Pacific collection not only because of their age and condition but also because they had journeyed

Figure 1. Green Dress, UBC Museum of Anthropology, Accession#3050/1. Courtesy of UBC Museum of Anthropology.

from the Pacific to Europe and then to Canada. They were also related to an individual, the Reverend John Williams, an English missionary who voyaged to the Pacific in 1817, accompanied by his wife Mary. He was considered one of the more talented and resourceful of missionaries – a godly mechanic. He began the practice of recruiting islanders as native teachers and built his own ship, the *Messenger of Peace*, so he could travel throughout the Pacific to monitor their "progress". He supervised the building of roads and churches, raised money by writing books chronicling his endeavours, and became a well-known public figure, giving talks throughout England, and never missing an opportunity to lobby the wealthy for funds to commission a new ship and continue his mission. His murder was considered newsworthy; he was a hero, a martyr, murdered whilst attempting to bring Christianity to the "heathens". His martyrdom secured him a place in history, and his name is still well known on the islands where he set up missions.

During his travels he amassed a collection of artefacts; some were deposited with the London Missionary Society, the family kept a few, and the rest were given to friends and acquaintances. The five donated to MOA are some of the oldest Pacific Islands objects to be found in a Canadian collection, which has some cachet in the museum world. However, it was of particular interest to me that the collection belonged to a time when colonial and evangelical expansion across the Pacific was beginning to ramp up, and I wondered how these objects might contribute in some way to contemporary discussions about this complicated and contested period. Surely there was some reason for their appearance at this particular time. Their very existence and the need to document them were sufficient to raise interest in the story of John Williams, and although this line of enquiry would position them in the historical record, I remained intrigued, perhaps obsessed, by the fact that they physically existed in the present, as did Williams' descendants and the descendants of those responsible for his death. Was it time for both sets of descendants, linked as they were by a single tragic event, to meet each other? And if they did agree to meet, what form would this meeting take? Did such things happen in Vanuatu? The donor, Michael Williams, one of Williams' many descendants living in western Canada, was also interested in these questions and willing to introduce me to the rest of the family to find out whether they were too. The response was mixed. Some viewed a possible meeting as an opportunity to reconnect with the history of their family and with each other, others less so. David Williams said, "I saw it as a way to possibly come to terms with certain interior intellectual conflicts over the nature of the missionary enterprise and its role in the colonial era, which I had come to regard negatively" (personal communication, 20 August, 2011). On Erromango the response was also mixed. Some thought that atonement for sins had already been given through conversion to Christianity and that there was no need to revisit old ground. Others viewed it as an opportunity to lift the so-called "curse" that was believed to have been placed on Erromango since John Williams' death. The curse of Martyr Island, a moniker for Erromango, was well known (see Robertson 1903). Ralph Regenvanu, then Director of the Vanuatu National Cultural Council, said, "I heard there was a curse because of killing the missionaries. It was talked about in terms of why they [the Erromangans] wouldn't be able to do certain things, or

Figure 2. Reconciliation Ceremony. Photograph by Ken Mayer, 20 November 2009.

succeed in getting certain aspects of culture revitalized" (personal communication, 4 March, 2012). He advised the Williams family to write to the Council of Chiefs and church leaders expressing their willingness to come to Erromango. If agreement were reached, then the family would be invited to attend a reconciliation ceremony in Erromango on 20 November 2009, the 170th anniversary of Williams' death.

Eighteen members of the Williams family travelled from Canada, England and South Africa to attend the ceremony. Before leaving, they expressed concern about what they should wear to be respectful, and requested information about local custom and what would be expected of them. I became their conduit for information and served as the liaison between them, the museum, contacts in Vanuatu, film crews, travel agents and other interested parties. When the family arrived in Port Vila, Chief Daniel Dan of Umponyelogi, Erromango greeted them along with representatives of the Erromango community living in Port Vila. Among them was Jocelyn Natgo who, unbeknownst to the Williams family and those accompanying them (including me), took their measurements so that she could organise the making of matching green dresses and shirts. The colour was incidental; she simply liked the shade of green. It is *kastom* (local practice) in Vanuatu for groups of people to wear the same attire for important events; the word had already gone out on Erromango for the women to wear the white *aelan dres* reserved for church-going and the men to wear white shirts and dark trousers. When the family arrived in Dillon's Bay on Erromango they were surprised and pleased that they could be identified by their green "reconciliation wear".

The complexity of the two days of events and ceremonies cannot possibly be described adequately in this short paper, so events related to the green dress are emphasised (see also Mayer 2009; Mayer, Naupa and Warri 2013). Members of the Williams family were seated on pews brought from the church, and the ni-Vanuatu dignitaries were seated adjacent to them. The programme began with prayers spoken by Pastor Obed Moses, followed by a speech of welcome from Chief William Mete, and responded to by the elders of the Williams family. Even though I placed myself on the periphery amongst the villagers, there to witness the procedures, I was inserted into the proceedings by being invited to the stage to tell the story of how a donation to a museum instigated a three-year process that led to this day. Speeches, prayers, an exchange of gifts and a welcome song penned by Annie Tahumpri, the local schoolteacher, were followed by two re-enactments: the 1839 death of John Williams and his assistant James Harris, and the deaths of Canadian missionary Reverend George Gordon and his wife Ellen in 1861, and his brother James in 1872. The deaths of all these missionaries led to Erromango's reputation as Martyr Island. The bodies and faces of the villagers participating in the re-enactment were stained black to signify their state of darkness before Christianity brought them into the light. The combination of their warrior clothing, threatening behaviour and brandishing of weapons also emphasised their pre-Christian reputation as warriors. The ni-Vanuatu acting as Williams, Harris and the Gordons were dressed as missionaries in white shirts and dark trousers, echoing the clothing of the dignitaries and church elders present. As Williams and Harris walked up the beach, Harris turned to Williams and said, "I think I have no peace in my heart – I think we are going to meet some challenges up there". He was right. They were attacked and killed and then dragged to the centre of the village where the warriors and the villagers joined together to sing the John Williams hymn, which is in the Presbyterian church song book and always sung on the anniversary of Williams' murder. The re-enactment was followed by the reconciliation ceremony, during which members of the clans responsible for the deaths of Williams, Harris and the Gordons came forward in groups to express their contrition, sometimes by a shaking of the hand and sometimes by tearful and heartrending admonitions. The family was unprepared for this and stood mute until one family member, Charles Milner Williams, stood forward and said, "People of Erromango, enough! Please, enough! There is nothing to forgive, but we, the family of the Reverend Williams, forgive you". The rest of the family followed him into the kneeling group and hugged them – the Williams' green dresses and shirts mingled with the villagers' white dresses and shirts.

Concerns about whether Charles had done the right thing were allayed at the end of the evening by Ralph Regenvanu, who said what Charles did "was perfect in terms of what you should do according to traditional protocols. He did just the right thing. No one told him. It was a universal understanding of what you

Figure 3. Installation at the UBC Museum of Anthropology. Photograph by Ken Mayer.

have to do in that situation". The ceremony culminated with William Natgo, one of the descendants of the clan who killed Williams, and his wife Titawa stepping forward and giving their seven-year-old daughter Uarai Jaylene Natgo, dressed in white with a white garland around her head, to the Williams family. On behalf of the family, Michael Williams and Charles Milner Williams stepped forward, accepted her as their goddaughter and gave her another name, Mary, in honour of John Williams' wife. Sempet Naritantop, custom advisor to the Simanlou Council of Chiefs, explained, "The Natgo family asked me what to do in custom to request forgiveness. Blood for blood, we gave a life for a life, that is our custom. We gave a female so that the receiving clan can be ensured future generations to make up for the life lost" (Mayer, Naupa and Warri 2013, 85). Some weeks later Jaylene's mother said, "It was God's will. Jaylene was a very sickly baby and we never thought she would survive infancy, but on that day I realized that her life had a greater purpose, that she was to seal the reconciliation between our family and the Williams family" (personal communication, December 2009). The two families are now inextricably linked and a few months later the Williams set up a small foundation to contribute towards Mary's education. The Williams family has also sent medical supplies to the village dispensary and is currently working on raising funds for new bookshelves for the local school library.

In 2010, a permanent exhibition was installed at MOA, which tells this story and includes the original donated artefacts alongside the newer objects relating to the reconciliation ceremony: the programmes prepared for the ceremony and church service, a duplicate of the medal given to older members of the Williams family, gifts given to the family, and a green shirt donated by a member of the film crew. My green dress had not yet been donated. This installation was announced in the Vanuatu national newspaper, the *Daily Post*, as an important event deserving international recognition. Nobody in the Williams family was willing to donate their green dresses or shirts to MOA, seemingly because, for them, these were the only tangible evidence they had of the reconciliation ceremony. Although I am not a member of the Williams family, I thought the donation of my dress would suffice as physical evidence of the museum's involvement in the realisation of the reconciliation ceremony. It is not usual for a curator to be so closely linked to a museum object, and it did take almost four years and the publishing of a book containing the story of the ceremony (Mayer, Naupa and Warri 2013) before I could let it go. MOA is now the only public repository in Canada for objects associated with John Williams, and amongst these is my green dress, speaking to memories and relationships not contained by the Museum but still part of the lives of communities in Canada and Erromango.

Interview

Greg Semu and Jacqueline Charles-Rault

Greg Semu is an independent researcher, curator and artist who has exhibited his work globally. Born in New Zealand, Greg Semu embraces Samoa as his ancestral and spiritual home. A theme that runs strongly through his work is cultural displacement, colonial impact on indigenous, particularly Pacific Islands, cultures and Christian religious iconography's mutation of tribal icons. In 2007, Semu was awarded the inaugural artist in residence position at the Museé du quai Branly, Paris, and created *The Battle of the Noble Savage* series. In 2010, the Tjibaou Cultural Centre in New Caledonia commissioned Semu to create *The Last Cannibal Supper, 'Cause Tomorrow We Become Christians,* a politically and historically significant work that explores the dictatorship of Christianity onto "primitive" tribes. In 2013, he was the winner of the People's Choice Award for the 62nd Blake Prize, with his video installation *Te Upoko o Hoani te Kaiiriiri, The Head of John the Baptist,* 2013.

JCR: "The Last Cannibal Supper ..... cause tomorrow we become Christians" (2010) is a fragmented series of work intertwined with religious iconography that consists of a series of images, which include two reinterpretations of "The last Supper" by Leonardo Da Vinci, one of which is an auto-portrait (Figure 1). There are also four close-up images depicting the twelve disciples present at the last supper with Christ in groups of three, as well as two "Piétà" images of , one of which is an auto-portrait, and two other images, entitled "The Assassination of Atai" and "Sacrifice for Glory". When you started work on this series did you start with the reinterpretation of the Leonardo Da Vinci painting "The Last Supper" and then add the other parts?

GS: The Last Supper is a childhood memory of a large, cheap, factory-made wall hanging that occupied most of the geography above an unused and blocked up fireplace. Everything seemed to gravitate around this ornamental centre piece in the living room, with its imitation wall rug, which was composed of synthetic materials and comprised of a highly toxic composition and electric colours.

Figure 1. Greg Semu. ***The Last Cannibal Supper... cause tomorrow we become Christians.*** **Auto Portrait with Twelve Disciples. 2010. Digital C-Type Print. 100 x 286cm.** Image courtesy of the Artist and Alcaston Gallery, Melbourne.

As an infant, I was often left alone to entertain myself, which I did by staring at the random scattering of framed family photos that acted like satellites circling a planet [the wall hanging reproducing The Last Supper]. They were like little pretext stories playing support to a massive drama that unfolded on the wall hanging as a gathering of predominantly men, punctuated with a few androgynous figures of questionable gender. As a lost child, I would visit the details of this fake velvet like painting and wonder: What liquids of crimson are housed in those glass goblets? Is that random bits of bread strewn? I'd look at the table legs and ask why are there so many sandaled feet? I'd look too at the wallpaper, the ceiling and wonder what the landscape was like outside of the trinity windows. Who are these people and what is the special occasion for such a big table? The wall hanging was preceded by family portraits of uncles, aunties, brothers, sisters and a young mum and dad in love and blessed with youth and potential. I'd ask myself, 'How does all of this synchronize? And why are there no pictures of me being celebrated on this trophy wall?' Fragments of a dream perhaps, as I regularly fell asleep gazing into the textured 'scène'. Da Vinci's masterpiece is the blueprint, which I built upon in the road leading up to the creation of the cannibal interpretation.

Da Vinci is the Archetype, and will always be credited as the 'Godfather' of all 'last suppers' the alpha omega, the genesis of an iconic Christian brand that resonates with believers and non-believers alike.

JCR: How important is your family's religion to you?

GS: My family and I don't share the same values regarding religious devotion. One member might consider it as precious and the other unimportant. My personal interpretation is that 'religion' in certain hands is a weapon of mass discipline, clumsy, blunt, destructive and fragile and easy to abuse. Fear, guilt and shame fused with physical punishment are all valid psychological arsenals that are effective and powerful in their use of persuasion. I speak only for myself. No doubt there are many benefits, that include: community engagement, healthy food habits (particular to the denomination we practiced), a personal sense of morality and respect towards our brothers, sisters, neighbours and strangers, which are all basic humanitarian traits for fostering harmonious living, but which are obviously not uniquely reserved for only religious practitioners. I do not reject my family's religion in any sense.

JCR: Residencies in different places and countries have become a part of your art practice over the past few years. "The Last Cannibal Supper .... cause tomorrow we become Christians" was created during your residency in New Caledonia in 2010 at the Tjibaou Cultural Centre with the indigenous people of New Caledonia, the Kanaks. How do international residencies influence your work practice and in particular your residency in New Caledonia at The Centre Cultural Jean-Marie Tjibaou – ADCK [Agency for the Development of Kanak Culture]?

GS: International residencies provide a plethora of platforms for cultural and artistic exchange. My preferred methodology is to insist on indigenous community engagement. I find my sources in research archives and libraries for historical evidence of the indigenous community's colonial experience, traditions and customs and then incorporate them into a photographic production, which opens a visual discourse inviting past and present issues surrounding conversations on the dilemmas and dichotomy in modern currencies.

The Centre Cultural Jean-Marie Tjibaou – ADCK is an amazing institution that provides the opportunity for integration. The artwork is the catalyst and becomes the vehicle for the participation of the Kanak tribesmen and women of New Caledonia, which is currently French, colonized. The namesake of the centre of Jean-Marie Tjibaou's legacy brought tears to my eyes as I read his story. A man similar, if not equal, to Mahatma Gandhi in his convictions for passive resistance and a free self-governed Nouméa, which unfortunately he was unable to follow through, due to a tragic twist of fate and political betrayal resulting in his assassination.

JCR: By looking at different religions and the theme of Christianity in the series "The Last Cannibal Supper", how did you associate all of your photographic images and in particular "Chief Ataï's Head", an interpretation of the 1878 beheading of the Kanak chief Ataï who fought the French colonial forces?

GS: The Last Cannibal supper is broken down systematically into a series: four images detailing three apostles at a time,-four comprising of the twelve disciples, plus the main feast (Figure 1), which has two versions. The second version includes a self-portrait for various reasons amongst them, economizing and capitalizing on this rare occasion.

Research during the residency revealed 'cannibalism' as a pre-colonial ritual custom that was once practiced by the Kanak of New Caledonia. Hence the title and parody intertwined with humour and history. The savage act of cannibalism when compared to the symbolic gestures made when covenanting with Christ is no doubt a cannibalistic metaphor. This bread is thy body, this wine is thy blood. The images of "La Pietà" were natural progressions on the theme of Christian iconography. "The Assassination of Atai" is unique to the Kanak colonial experience and is well recorded and documented in the history books of both indigenous genealogies and the French colonial resistance. Ataï was beheaded and gifted to the French as an ultimatum to the survival of the many villagers in the district that chief Ataï was defending. The head of Ataï was for a long time hidden in the vast collections of French museum institutions and thought to be lost or stolen. [It was found in July 2011 and negotiations are underway for its return to New Caledonia.] I parallel the assassination of chief Ataï to the biblical story "The head of John the Baptist", a rebel, whose head was beheaded and gifted. I pay homage to a man who forfeited his life for freedom. I am fascinated with the phenomenology of decapitation and albeit savage tribal acts of brutality or an act of justice enforced by a court of law, government or dictatorship.

JCR: Is your self-portrait as Christ in "The Last Cannibal Supper" wearing a Samoan *tatau* or *Pe'a* in fact a statement that references your Samoan heritage and tattoo?

GS: Yes! It is the most unique and original statement that I am privileged to make. Christ with Samoan *tatau*. It is a collision of iconographic symbols. Christianity is estimated at 2000 years to the birth of Christ and prior to that based on the esoteric. The Samoan *tatau* pre-dates Christ by several thousand years. I cannot give you any evidence that supports this as factual, as I'm merely regurgitating numbers gleamed from numerous conversations on Polynesian origins and migrations, but it fluctuates between 3 and 5 thousand years in the Pacific! The significance of the age of Samoan *tatau* is profoundly important. A living, cultural tradition that can retrospectively trace an un-broken genealogical line from that moment is momentous! It's equivalent to the miracles of the Pyramids, the Aztecs and Incas, or as relevant and mystical as the great religious texts of the old and new testaments, the Torah, the Koran and the secret scrolls. The *tatau* is an encryption, which is chiselled on to the human body. One of its many purposes is as a 'passport to Pulotu'. Pulotu is the underworld in the afterlife. In Pulotu there are two levels of heaven, one for the commoner, and the other for the elite and the high chiefs. Entry is permitted only to bearers of the *tatau*. Christ in the garden of Gethsemane bled from every pore of his body and the pain endured is associated with a covenant made with God. The *tatau* is also a covenant sealed with blood and pain. A bond made with the *Atua* [gods]'s and *aiga* [family].

JCR: How did the Kanak actors feel about re-enacting "The Last Cannibal Supper" with you?

GS: I cannot speak or imagine on behalf of the indigenous cast. The "Casting sauvage" or street casting's final ensemble was a cocktail of experienced dancers/ performers and a recognized cultural dance troop. The works are sensitive. They weave a fine and fierce dance between blasphemous profanity, or not? The cast are specialists in their field, and professional in their conduct, commissioned to participate in a unique Greg Semu community arts project, which is an artistic act of provocation. Nonetheless it's difficult not to be engaged personally. For a nanosecond, it was a life changing moment for me. Shifting paradigms internally through the language of art by asking 'could you imagine being empowered?' brought us to the crucial key element, which was 'the dreaming'. Re-examine the evidence presented by colonial historical recordings that have been published, archived, have yet to be discovered, or, likewise, pardon, recreate and imagine self-empowering alternative interpretations contrary to the status quo propaganda. The experience, the process, the interaction and the exchange of the collective effort of the cast crew and pre-production on the shoot day followed by 'What if?'. I can only hope that it was a positive building exercise for everyone who participated, both personally and professionally, rewarded by a small financial gesture for their skills, time and energy.

JCR: Do you think having had a Samoan *tatau* has made you connect more to your own Samoan heritage?

GS: Yes, in a private and subtle manner. What is it like to feel human? The *tatau* is a gift embedded uniquely for each person, a shared heritage, which is experienced and expressed individually.

JCR: How do Samoans respond to your work?

GS: Obviously, I don't really know! I imagine there are many Samoans who will resonate and defend my work and many more that will be offended and condemn it. They'll be individually expressing shared internal dialogues of ethnicity and origin. Is there a sense of belonging that defines the boundaries of displacement or the ambiguity of identity? I focus on inclusivity. Look for themes that are common between social groups, as the more defined the cultural details, the more exclusive and isolated they become. Samoan culture is very strong. It grew during the 1970s in Auckland NZ and the cultural boundaries were acute and territorial. It's a result of urbanization and industrial migrations from satellite island nations to the metropolis. Inter-relations are healthier today. My primary audience would not be Samoan, as it would be like preaching to the converted. In 2000, I was invited to exhibit at the 5th Biennale de Lyon/'partage des Exotisms' curated by Jean Hubert Martin, as one of 120 artists from around the world. The work "Body of Christ in 12 parts" is a self-portrait with cross as Christ. Selected by one of the main sponsors as a hero publicity image for the biennale it was subsequently banned from being printed in five newspapers from five European countries, due to its sensitive iconographic content, an old dialogue of the devotional and the diabolical.

JCR: There's a very romantic quality to your rendition of "La Pietà" was this a deliberate choice?

GS: I'm mesmerized by the drama and beauty of suffering. How a tragedy brings people together for a nanosecond of compassion, humanity, loss and hope. I was fascinated by the illustrations contained in the black glossy textured covered paper tombs of the Bible and other various literatures. Instantly transported from the mundane ceremonial dogma of worship and adoration, I studied the minute detail and facial expressions and body language, the metallic armed helmet wearing guards with their swords and spears poised for death and the Romanesque pillars and concrete constructions of ancient empires. These were filled with hundreds and thousands of inhabitants that held my attention during the church sermons and hymns every Sunday. I could not read, so the illustrious pictures and the thin translucent texture of the sacred printed paper page was an oasis in a tsunami of endless text amid the heavy air of the gathered faithful. Both Pietà are based on paintings on display at the Louvre, in Paris, France. They are fragmented dreams as I slept with the drone of preaching and praising amongst an audible background. I cannot explain the obsession with European paintings and religious iconography. I don't over think the work that gets made. As a creature of habit, I only have one or two conversations and I just keep repeating and evolving the dialogue until I reach saturation of the divine.

Part Three

Curios?

Moffat's model house, South Africa

Catherine Elliott Weinberg

The British Museum is custodian of a scale model of a typical nineteenth-century Tswana house, formerly in the London Missionary Society (LMS) Museum. Presumably made sometime between 1818 and 1826 by Scottish-born pioneer missionary to South Africa, Robert Moffat (1795–1883) of the LMS, this object raises a number of questions. Why was it made and what purpose was it meant to serve? How was it once understood – why did it appear under the guise of a New Zealand Māori house in an early illustration (Craik 1830) – and how can it be interpreted today?

The 1826 catalogue of the LMS Museum indicates that a "MODEL of a HOUSE at Lattakoo" (LMS 1826, 46), almost certainly Moffat's, was on display. From its early beginnings, the Museum collection grew and in 1835 it relocated along with the LMS headquarters to Blomfield Street, Finsbury (London) (Wingfield 2012, 115). As shown in a number of illustrations of the LMS Museum published in the popular press of the day, by the mid-nineteenth century the model house, encased in a small vitrine, occupied a prime place in the middle of the main exhibition area (see Introduction Figure 1). It stood next to the centrepiece, a stuffed giraffe, also from South Africa (see Wingfield, this volume). A later catalogue of the LMS Museum provides more detail about the model, attributing it to Robert Moffat, and describing it as "An exact model of a Bechuana [Tswana] house, made on the spot" (LMS n.d., 37).

That "spot", as recorded by the LMS catalogue entry of 1826, was the settlement of Lattakoo.[35] The actual site of Lattakoo is somewhat elusive as it changed location several times during the nineteenth century. In 1817, Lattakoo moved a relatively short distance from present-day Dithakong westward to Maruping (both settlements in the Kuruman area of the Northern Cape). "New Lattakoo" (Maruping), which simply became known as Lattakoo (Schoeman 1995, 78) and then Kuruman (Schapera 1951, xvi), was the capital of *Kgosi* (chief) Mothibi of the Tlhaping, the southernmost Tswana group. Near Lattakoo was the LMS's mission to the Tlhaping, which the young Moffat first visited in September 1818

Figure 1. Model of a Tswana house, h. 21cm x w. 41.5cm x d. 32.5cm (British Museum Af,LMS.3). Photograph by Mike Row. Courtesy of the Trustees of the British Museum.

35 Spellings vary.

and which from 1821 became his home until he returned for good to Britain in 1870. Although he did not establish the original mission, it has become known as "Moffat Mission" and is strongly associated his life's work, and that of his wife Mary, among the Tswana people.

The sheer size of Lattakoo and its distinctive architecture struck early European visitors, some of whom felt compelled to depict and describe the settlement and its dwellings. Moffat was no exception. Despite his sketchy formal education and apparent lack of enthusiasm for writing, Moffat – the former gardener who would go on to master the Tswana language and translate the Bible into that tongue – has left us several accounts of Lattakoo, including this remarkable model. It is possible that the practically inclined Moffat, who was good with his hands, made the model in order to think through and describe what he observed.

Although Moffat's Tswana house, rendered in miniature, does not afford a view inside the structure (the roof is not removable and the doorway is narrow), it is not a superficial first-hand account. Indeed, he included the space immediately around the dwelling, the *lelapa* (courtyard living areas encircling the house) enclosed by fencing, which is in many respects "the real home" (Walton 1956, 52). Moffat also took care to include a scale on the board as well as several paper labels, mostly now only partially legible. Each of the two small, concave circular fireplaces within the screened-off area is labelled. He omitted the other fence that is usually part of the dwelling, instead indicating its position with labels, perhaps so as not to obscure completely the veranda with its wooden pillars and the cylindrical mud wall within.

While at the Cape, Moffat was to live in a succession of dwellings, often described as "huts", before he had a more conventional settler-style house built on the site that became the permanent mission station at Kuruman. In his *Missionary Labours and Scenes in Southern Africa* (1842), Moffat describes having "seen houses built of all descriptions" during his sojourn and having "assisted in the construction of a good many" (R. Moffat 1842, 104). With regard to the Tswana cone-on-cylinder style dwellings, Moffat expressed concern that they were "entirely the work of the women", given the hard and dangerous labour involved. However, he conceded that the houses, "though temporary, and requiring great labour to keep them constantly in repair, are nevertheless very well adapted to the climate" (R. Moffat 1842, 252). Moffat's appreciation and knowledge of indigenous craftsmanship may have inspired the model, as well as the temporary replacement "dwelling-house" he built for himself and his family shortly after arriving at the mission. In many respects, his own house seems to have been inspired by local architecture and to have adopted elements of local construction. Moffat (in Schapera 1951, 59) describes it as follows:

> *The roof is supported by pillars formed of rough trunks of a hardy sort of tree. The wall, composed of reed and clay, is formed in the inside of the pillars... The massive pillars, sunk a suitable length into the ground, enables* [sic] *the house to remain immovable amidst the devastating thunderstorms which we often experience in this part of Africa.*

Anthropologist Isaac Schapera (1951, xxv) criticises Moffat for not describing the culture of the people among whom he worked, making the missionary, in his opinion, of only limited use as an ethnographer. However, in creating the model, Moffat seems to have perceived the centrality of the house within Tswana culture. It should be noted that at that time, houses were the "primary units of production and property" (Comaroff and Comaroff 1991, 133) and the "outstanding social unit was the household" (Schapera 1951, xx). In the case of wealthier individuals, each wife within a polygamous marriage would have had her own dwelling. Typically, a household compound comprised a cluster of houses, each with its own front and back courtyard, bounded by fencing. Lattakoo would have been made up of many such households. The vernacular houses there, with their front and back courtyard layout, are said to have been typical of all Tswana houses in the nineteenth century (Steyn 2011, 105).

Moffat, clearly inspired by the local houses, may have made the model with the LMS Museum in mind. He was certainly aware of the Museum and had experienced the impact of its exhibits. In a letter written to his parents shortly before his departure for South Africa in 1816, Moffat describes spending "some time in viewing the museum" (then at Old Jewry, London) and how the "curiosities" on display there, specifically "the objects of pagan worship", strengthened his resolve to become a missionary among fellow "beloved mortals" (J. S. Moffat 1890, 19). Formally established in 1814, the Museum displayed man-made objects and natural history specimens, many of which were sent to the LMS by its missionaries abroad (See Nuku and Wingfield, this volume). In exhibiting these items the intention seems to have been to showcase the work of the missionaries – their challenges and successes, especially in terms of "trophies of Christianity" (Seton 2012, 99) – as well as the handiwork of missionised peoples.

Once at the LMS Museum, the model would have joined the other "curiosities" on display. We know something of its reception and use at the LMS Museum thanks to literary scholar George Lillie Craik (1789–1866), a Scotsman who first visited London in 1824 before settling there in 1826. As noted on the later British Museum registration documentation, Craik included an engraving of the model in his *The New Zealanders,* where it is mistakenly described as a "New Zealand Hut and Fence of Garden" (1830, 157). Published in 1830 by the *Society for the Diffusion of Useful Knowledge*, Craik's book was one in a series intended as an affordable source of self-improvement; entertaining yet worthwhile information aimed at a working to middle class audience. Craik does not appear to have travelled to New Zealand, gathering instead information about Māori material culture from missionary and other museum collections. Given the popularity of the LMS Museum's (apparently often unlabelled) exhibits at that time, particularly the Polynesian material, it is perhaps unsurprising that an illustration of Moffat's model appears in this mistaken guise.

Aside from its prominent position within the exhibit, the model was furthermore included in the part of the LMS collection that was transferred as a permanent loan to the British Museum (BM) in 1890, after much persuasion and persistence on the part of the BM. The British Museum's Keeper, A.W. Franks (1826–1897), recognised the importance of the collection. Franks was instrumental in obtaining for the BM what he thought to be the most significant aspects of the LMS Museum assemblage. The BM later purchased the loan material in 1911. Attribution of the model to Moffat is reiterated in the BM's documentation. The object's registration slip, echoing the later LMS Museum catalogue (LMS n.d., 37), describes it as a "South African hut Bechuana[n?] made on the spot by Dr Moffat". Once at the BM, Moffat's authorship was of lesser importance and the model house was, until more recently and until the present research, described as "Tswana [made]".

An embodiment of the early Tswana and missionary encounter, the model may be seen as emblematic of the missionary himself and of Tswana culture. Moffat was evidently inspired by the workmanship of Tswana architecture and in making the model he sought to produce knowledge about the Tswana people. Arguably he recognised the significance and centrality of the house in Tswana culture, despite being critical of that culture in other respects. Moffat's name, which according to Schapera (1951, xiii) is "illustriously associated" with the Kuruman mission and his work among the Tlhaping, can once again be firmly linked to this model Tswana house.

Acknowledgements

The author wishes to thank Joanne Ichimura (Archives and Special Collections, SOAS Library) for her assistance as well as, at the British Museum, Lissant Bolton, Chris Spring and Julie Hudson (Department of Africa, Oceania and the Americas), Mike Row (for photography) and Verena Kotonski (Department of Conservation and Scientific Research).

Wooden doll, Fiji

Karen Jacobs

This wooden doll (Figure 1) dressed in a plaited fibre skirt is part of a collection associated with the Reverend Richard Burdsall Lyth, who worked as a Methodist missionary and medical doctor in Fiji between 1839 and 1845 – a pioneering time in Fiji's mission history, before the 1854 conversion to Christianity of Ratu Seru Cakobau, the most powerful chief in Fiji. The doll has articulated limbs and measures 25.7cm in height. The eyes are painted white, with black pupils, and the lips painted red. The elbow joints are fixed with pegs; the lower legs are attached at the knee with metal wire. The hands have a distinctive splayed form and there are traces of hair, probably human, on the head. The doll, which is clearly intended to be female, though anatomical details are not shown, wears a necklace and armlet made of trade beads.

The doll is part of a series of three dolls in the Lyth collection at the Fiji Museum, all dressed in Fijian clothing. While this doll has been clothed with a *liku* skirt made of *vau* (*Hibiscus tiliaceous* fibre), the other dolls have been wrapped in sheets of bark cloth (*masi* and *gatu*, made of the inner bark of the paper mulberry, *Broussonetia papyrifera*). One is made to resemble "a chief", as the museum's register reveals, while the other is dressed as a "woman of rank" (Figure 2). The dolls entered the Fiji Museum in 1958 after the Museum's curator R. A. Derrick had located the collection in England, where it was still in the possession of the Lyth family. He arranged the collection's transfer to the museum with descendant Philip Lyth. This transfer was accompanied by several newspaper articles – all by the same author, Terry Farnfield (1958a, 1958b, 1958c) – stating that the collection was valuable as a remnant of pre-Christian Fiji. The dolls, in particular, caught the author's attention:

> *No longer do Fiji craftsmen make the wooden dolls with articulated limbs, such as Dr. Lyth collected. Fijian children now have to get along with plastic dolls. The dolls which Dr. Lyth took home to England were almost certainly made for a chieftain's daughter.* (Farnfield 1958a: 17)

The author, lamenting the fact that wooden dolls have been replaced with plastic versions, assumes that the practice of making dolls was a generic custom for Fijians. However, dolls were not usual Fijian products, though wooden

Figure 1. Doll, collected by Reverend Richard Burdsall Lyth (Fiji Museum 58.18). Photograph by Karen Jacobs, 2014.

images were. This raises the question as to who made these dolls, and where? The dolls' heads could be considered to correspond to a known Fijian style, with a disproportionately large head and small features in the lower face area, but they are not directly comparable to pre-Christian Fijian images. The dolls' limbs are fixed with pegs, which is not an indigenous Fijian technique – though the peg technique was used on nineteenth-century New Zealand Māori puppets. The wire attachments may be a later repair as wooden pegs are visible in the upper legs. The dolls' clothing is an accurate representation of early nineteenth-century Fijian ceremonial dress.

While doing research on Fijian human sculpture in the 1950s, Karl Erik Larsson came across the dolls and assumed they were made in Fiji. He sent a photograph of them to the Keeper of the Bethnal Green Museum in London, who thought the dolls' heads were non-European, while the body was European, and so suspected they were a Fijian product of European inspiration. Larsson therefore concluded that the dolls were made in Fiji under missionary influence (Larsson 1960, 104-5). However, when I showed a photograph to doll expert Bunny Campione in 2013, she immediately recognised the dolls as Grodnertal wooden peg dolls. Interestingly, these dolls were made in Austria and then shipped abroad to be dressed in local clothing. Representing adults rather than children, their costumes were intended to be as authentic as possible through the use of local fabrics. This would explain the accuracy of the Fijian clothing. Further research corroborates the assumption that the doll in question is likely to be a wooden peg-jointed doll made by German or Tyrolean toymakers. Hand-carved in pine, poplar or maple, these dolls are characterised by slender necks, sloping shoulders, hourglass figures and splayed hands. The limbs were jointed at the shoulders, elbows, hips and knees. Similar dolls were later made in New England, where they came to be known as Penny Woodens, as they sold in the mid-nineteenth century for a penny. Usually about 10cm in height, dolls could measure up to 30cm. The larger dolls were not only more expensive, but also had elaborate coiffures (Christopher 1971, 254).

The fact that an expensive doll reached Fiji and was dressed locally, then taken to the UK, where it became a family heirloom, and eventually returned to Fiji as a "cannibal day relic[s]" (Farnfield 1958b) is an extraordinary story that bears witness to the movements of objects collected by missionaries, their value to descendants and the changing connotations associated with these objects. The doll also provides us with a rare glimpse of missionary domestic life with all its contradictions and complexities.

Richard Burdsall Lyth (1810–1887) was ordained as a minister of the Methodist Church on 30 September 1836 and was elected to serve as a missionary in the Wesleyan Methodist Missionary Society. In the same year, he married Mary Ann

Figure 2. Dolls on display in the exhibition *Art and the Body: Exploring the Role of Clothing in Fiji at the Fiji Museum* (March–May 2014). Left to right, according to museum registration: "dressed as a young girl" (58.18), "dressed as a chief" (58.16), "dressed as a lady of rank" (58.17). The liku skirt, displayed underneath, was also collected by Reverend Lyth (58.1). Photograph by Karen Jacobs.

Lyth (née Hardy, 1811–1890) and in October they sailed to Tonga to take up post. In 1838, they were transferred to a new appointment in Fiji, where they stayed for fifteen years. The Wesleyan Missionary Society expected its agents to remain in the field for long periods, only returning early in case of ill health. A single missionary serving in the Pacific region was only allowed to return to England for a year (to find a wife) after he had completed ten years of service (Warren 1827, 194-5). This meant that missionaries were separated from their extended families for most of their lives and had to adjust to a different climate and lifestyle, which they were also trying to change and "improve". Missionaries were expected to maintain exemplary behaviour. The mission household had to provide an example of the advantages of Christianity, to be copied by the local people (Heath 1987, 143). A missionary family thus had to lead by example.

The Lyths had nine children – four boys and five girls – but some died at an early age (John Conway, Richard Burdsall, and Elizabeth Ann). Their first child, John Conway, was born in 1837 during the journey to Tonga; he died in Fiji in 1839. The other children were all born in Fiji. The family adapted to a Fijian lifestyle to a certain extent by relying on local produce and by utilising Fijian material culture, but one way of leading by example was through the use of European goods. The supplies brought by the mission ships, *Triton* and *John Wesley*, provided different flavours and possessions and barter goods which could be exchanged for indigenous goods and services. Meanwhile, Fijian objects were sent home for fundraising purposes, as Mary Ann Lyth writes in a letter: "We are very much obliged for your kind presents the shawl and collar shall have great pleasure in wearing ... I was glad to hear that you received the box of curiosities safe".[36] Gradually, they accumulated European household goods, sent as gifts or in response to specific requests. The Lyth children played with European toys – building blocks, dolls, hoops, balls and their favourite toy, a Noah's ark (Heath 1987, 174). In one letter, Mary Ann Lyth discusses a particular doll that was given to them when they were based in Somosomo on the island of Taveuni, north-eastern Fiji:

> *Will you present our thanks to the Committee of the Juvenile Missionary Bazaar for their kind present to us... The Doll is the wonder and astonishment of Somosomo, and I can only produce it to a very select few – or we should have the house full all day long, to look at this child from Papalagi. When I shut her eyes I say go to sleep – they are sure the thing is alive.*[37]

The fact that it is called a "child from Papalagi" (Europe) suggests this doll was pale in colour. The reference to the closing of the eyes indicates the doll had "sleeping eyes". Dolls with eyes that opened and shut by means of a wire protruding from the side of the doll, or by pulling a string, appeared as early as the 1820s. However, the technique developed further and it was only by the end of the nineteenth century that white-coloured bisque or porcelain dolls with sleeping eyes became widespread (Christopher 1971, 219, 269-70). It is therefore unclear

36 Letter of Mary Ann Lyth to Mrs Jackson Brewery, 11 April 1842; courtesy Harry Lyth.

37 Letter of Mary Ann Lyth to Mrs Jackson Brewery, 8 May 1843; courtesy Harry Lyth.

whether this comment refers to the doll in question. The quote does show how regulated access to foreign goods was to Fijians. It is therefore likely that the doll that forms the topic of this chapter was used by the Lyth children rather than having been made for a Fijian chief's daughter. Who clothed the doll remains unknown, but the accuracy of dress suggests it was dressed by a Fijian. The *liku* would have been especially made for the doll; the barkcloth would have been cut from larger existing pieces.

Clothing was a means by which good Christian standards were demonstrated – local alternatives were not deemed suitable. Mary Ann Lyth's letters to her relatives in Britain often include an acknowledgement for received cloth and clothing, which was not just destined for the Lyth family and other Europeans but also for converted Fijians:

> *For the dresses from the Ladies Sewing Association we are very thankful. We have divided them amongst the District these are what our natives very much prize and in paying the women for washing or our servants there is nothing they like better. When we have them the women who live with us, we expect them to wear them continually, else they are naked to the waist – a most disgusting sight for us. But I am thankful to say that some of them Andi Vatea /the chiefs wife for one/ begin to feel ashamed to be uncovered and seldom appear without a dress of some sort or other.*[38]

Mary Ann Lyth expresses her unease with traditional Fijian clothing that consisted of a *liku* (skirt), leaving a woman's breasts bare. Traditionally, a Fijian girl would receive her first *liku* around the time of puberty, after she had received tattoos around the hips. On marrying, a woman wore a *liku* which entirely surrounded the body. After the birth of her first child, she wore a longer *liku*. As such, a woman's status could be read from her clothing. A multi-coloured and multi-layered *liku*, such as the doll is wearing, was reserved for chiefly women. The reference to shame by Mary Ann Lyth articulates differing values of dress. Fijian women would consider themselves fully dressed with their tattoo and *liku*. In the 1840s, explorer Wilkes (1845, 356) remarked that, "Though almost naked, these natives have a great idea of modesty, and consider it extremely indelicate to expose the whole person".

Interestingly, while being appalled by Fijian traditional dress, Mary Ann Lyth (or her children) possessed a doll representing this mode of clothing. The message is somewhat incongruous. It is likely that play with Fijian children was discouraged in missionary households (Figure 3), or that play was probably only allowed with the children of Fijian converts. Similar to other mission children, the Lyth children were sent to school in Auckland from 1849 onwards, to get them away from the undesirable influences of Fijian children (Lawry 1850, 45-6; see also Hooper, this volume). Paradoxically, the children were allowed to play with a representation of a pre-Christian Fijian woman in doll form. Is the doll a trophy, since the doll wears clothing that was strongly discouraged by missionaries? When the Lyth collection was transferred to the Fiji Museum in 1958, the dolls were mentioned in all three

38 Letter of Mary Ann Lyth from Viwa to Mrs John Jackson, 26 November 1847; courtesy Harry Lyth.

Figure 3. Sketch drawn in 1854 by Mary Ann Lyth of the mission premises at Lakeba, where the Lyth family was based for some years during their time in Fiji. Courtesy of Harry Lyth.

articles that discuss the collection's transfer. Each article gives the collection a specific status ranging from "art" associated with "cannibals" (Farnfield 1958a) to "cannibal day relics" (Farnfield 1958b) and "Fiji trophies" (Farnfield 1958c). The point is particularly poignant when we consider the further biography of the doll. If it was a toy for Lyth's daughters, why was it returned to the Fiji Museum as a Fijian item? By the 1950s the dolls appear to have lost their identity as European toys and had become Fijian artefacts, since the clothing was so clearly identifiable as Fijian. Perhaps it is more adequate to consider the doll as a representational embodiment of two worlds colliding; with a European-made body, and dressed in Fiji, the doll is a product of missionary encounter.

Acknowledgments

The author is grateful to Bunny Campione for invaluable advice and Harry Lyth for providing the Fijian Art Research Project Team (funded by AHRC) with transcripts of Richard and Mary Ann Lyth's letters and photographs of Mary Ann Lyth's sketchbook.

Drum, Torres Strait, Australia

Anita Herle

This magnificent Torres Strait Islander drum was acquired by the British Museum on 23 November in 1886. According to the registration slip, it "was made for Mr Macfarlane [*sic*] on Saibai Island". Alfred Haddon, the Cambridge-trained zoologist-cum-anthropologist who first went to the Torres Strait in 1888, was "informed by the natives that it was made, according to special instructions, through the chief of Saibai, for the Rev. Dr. S. Macfarlane [*sic*], just before that energetic missionary finally left the Torres Strait" (Haddon 1894, 42). A close examination of this drum, alongside the context of its collection, points to a series of personal and intercultural relations which combined to produce this unique object.

It is a particularly outstanding example of the *warup* style, characterised by the pronounced hourglass shape and manner of ornamentation (Haddon 1894, 39-43). Elegantly shaped and larger than most such drums, its bulbous head and shovel-like jaw accentuate the narrow "waistline". As with numerous other examples of this type, it is decorated with incised designs highlighted with lime infill and further embellished with cassowary feathers, ochre and goa nuts, which would produce a rattling sound when the drum was played. Yet this *warup* is unusual not only for its size and the extraordinary skill demonstrated by its creators, but because the incised decoration includes a more extensive and much broader range of design elements than typically seen.

Samuel McFarlane was originally sent to Lifu (then known as Lifou) in the Loyalty Islands, New Caledonia, by the London Missionary Society (LMS) in 1859 (Mullins and Wetherall 1996). Tensions between the French colonial administrators and the British meant that he was forced to leave the island, so he set about establishing a mission in New Guinea. On 1 July 1871 he arrived on Darnley Island in the north-eastern Torres Strait in the mission boat *Surprise.* McFarlane and the Rev. Archibald Murray were accompanied by eight Pacific Islander teachers from Lifu, the wives of those who were married, and four children (McFarlane 1888; Philp *in press* [2014]). This momentous encounter has been incorporated into Islander history as "the Coming of the Light", an event that continues to be marked by annual celebrations and re-enactments.

Figure 1. Torres Strait Islander warup drum from Saibai Island. Collected by Samuel McFarlane 1874–1886. British Museum Oc,+.3401. Courtesy of the Trustees of the British Museum.

The LMS teachers from the South Seas were placed on various islands throughout the Strait and McFarlane went on to establish a mission station on Mer, where he set up the Papuan Institute, composed of an industrial school and a teachers' seminary (McFarlane 1888, 87-91). The Institute on Mer attracted people from other islands in the Torres Strait and McFarlane used it as a base from which to travel throughout the region, visiting the growing number of mission stations and promoting the work of the LMS.

During his time as a missionary, McFarlane assembled a large collection of zoological specimens and a number of artefacts from the Torres Strait and New Guinea, many of which were sold to the British Museum via Edward Gerrard, a London taxidermist and dealer (Philp *in press* [2014]). Unlike many missionary collections assembled in Britain and used to promote the work of the Mission, McFarlane's primary motivation was to sell the material to raise money to support his wife and two children. They returned permanently to England in 1877, where McFarlane joined them after leaving the New Guinea mission in 1886. Unfortunately, there is no known written record by McFarlane describing the material he collected, but it is worth noting that, like this drum, the turtle-shell

Figure 2: Drawing of one of the motifs on the drum. This illustration is based on a drawing by Alfred Haddon, published as figure 45 on Plate III in Haddon (1894).

masks that he obtained from other Torres Strait islands are similarly outstanding, often unique, examples of their type. They demonstrate the skill and imagination of their producers and reflect the interests of McFarlane as a collector, no doubt keen to maximise the value of the collections he planned to sell.

Drums formed part of extensive trade relations between Torres Strait Islanders and people from the neighbouring regions of New Guinea, the source of the wood and cassowary feathers (Haddon 1894, 39). Both *warup* and the more streamlined *buruburu* drums were made from a single piece of hardwood, which was skilfully hollowed and shaped through a laborious procedure of burning and chiselling. Most Islander drums were made in New Guinea and modified in the Torres Strait, a process that often included the addition of personal markers such as incised designs representing the owner's totem. Some were given names and their custodianship passed down through families. Drums were extremely valuable and powerful objects, and it is still considered dangerous to walk in front of the mouth of a drum when it is being played.

The combination of what is known about the context of this drum's creation with an analysis of its overall composition points to a story of complex relations between Saibai Islanders, McFarlane, and the LMS. While the chief's special instructions for the creation of this drum remain obscure, a close examination of its incised decoration reveals many innovations in style and composition. Haddon considered the drum a "remarkably fine specimen" and "the largest I ever saw" (Haddon 1894, 42), yet he was somewhat dismissive of the drum's incised decoration, describing it as "crowded with various figures which, though of considerable interest from an artistic point of view, are quite out of place on a drum" (ibid). In his work on decorative art, Haddon (1894, 21-43, Plates 1, 3; 1895, 13-25; 1912, 364-73) isolated individual designs as a means of identifying the various animals represented and to use as comparative examples in his research on the evolution and distribution of art within the region.

Most of the animals depicted – cassowary, dog, crocodile, and turtle – are totems, typically used as personal markers in body decoration and on objects such as drums and bamboo tobacco pipes. The unprecedented inclusion of four distinct totems on a single *warup* indicates that this drum likely referred to several individuals or a larger group. Interestingly, the crocodile is shown alongside a series of its footprints, suggesting movement and a possible narrative. The bulbous section of the drum includes numerous human figures. Those on the side carry fish and crayfish, while a larger central figure holds up a turtle, likely referring to the species of green turtle that continues to be highly prized for feasting (Figure 2). Three medallions, each containing a human head in profile, are positioned along the topside of the *warup's* head. This novel design element is reminiscent of coins and may refer to the money paid for the drum or possibly offerings to the mission.

The lizard skin on the top of the *warup* also has a large red cross, a strong indication of conversion to Christianity. The surface of the lizard skin has small lumps of wax that were heated to tighten the tympanum and tune the instrument. This *warup* was made to be played and one can easily imagine it as part of the music and offerings of food that often accompanied church services and the arrival of visiting European missionaries. While the specific stories associated with this drum are unknown, it embodies a series of relationships and networks between Sabai Islanders, their trading partners in New Guinea, the LMS, McFarlane and his family. The creation of the drum, the implied narrative, and the bringing together of totems on a single object suggest the unifying force of the mission. Credited with bringing "the light" to the Torres Strait, the chief and people of Sabai demonstrated their good faith to McFarlane and ensured that he had something valuable to take back home.

Chess Piece, Botswana

Ceri Ashley

Perched on a low range of hills bordering the Kalahari in northern Botswana, an abandoned mission site was excavated between 2008 and 2009. Known as the Lake Ngami Mission, the site was established in 1893 by the London Missionary Society (LMS), and occupied by Alfred John Wookey, his family, and various assistants. Strung along the side of a hill, all that remains of this venture today are three stone house foundations, collapsed mud-brick walls, and scattered artefacts. Excavation at the largest of the houses revealed an unexpected wealth of things, attesting to everyday patterns of life, from diet and crockery to toys, jewellery and clothing. Amongst these is a chess pawn (Figure 1) providing a rare insight into the leisure hours of Wookey and his associates. Combining the archaeological evidence with evidence from their correspondence to the LMS in London suggests that this chess piece both represents a materialisation of the missionary ideal, and conversely, also stands as a symbol of the mission's failure a mere three years later.

Over the course of the nineteenth century, the LMS extended its influence deeper and deeper into Tswana society, with a string of LMS stations that reached as far north as Palapye by 1889 (See Lane, this volume). Lake Ngami, however, even further to the north and west, remained unsettled, despite being visited by David Livingstone in 1849 when he "discovered" the lake (Lovett 1899, 611). During this visit, the local Tswana chief, or *Kgosi,* Letsholathebe, pleaded with Livingstone to establish a mission amongst his people. LMS officials in London, however, feared for the costs and difficulties inherent in such a far-flung venture (Lovett 1899, 638). In 1877 and 1885, the Reverend James Hepburn returned to the area in an attempt to re-kindle interest, although he now found Letsholathebe's son, Moremi, less welcoming (Lovett 1899, 638). Nevertheless, in 1892, Wookey began the arduous journey to the Khwebe Hills, eventually arriving in August 1893 to establish the long-envisaged mission.

As was common practice, Wookey travelled to the Khwebe Hills with significant quantities of essential food supplies, equipment and personal effects. The archaeology reflects this; little or no locally produced material culture was found. Instead, an implausibly rich selection of glass, tin and china emerges,

Figure 1. Chess piece (height c. 2.1 cm) recovered during archaeological investigation of the Lake Ngami Mission. Artefact now stored at Botswana National Museum, Gaborone (Site code KWH1, context 11). Photograph by Ceri Ashley 2009.

materially ill-suited to either the long journey or the local conditions upon arrival. This incongruous assemblage perhaps reflects a natural preference for familiar staples (tea, sugar) so far from home. However, as Comaroff and Comaroff (1997) have eloquently argued, such behaviour was also part of a broader ideology of moral transformation through material and bodily practice. Clothes, ploughs and architecture, for example, were vehicles to radically transform notions of personhood, landscape and society, moving towards European ideas of rationalism, order and modesty, and away from a "corrupting" Tswana worldview. The seemingly mundane refuse of daily life at the Khwebe Hills thus becomes testament to a profound moral crusade.

The chess piece can be viewed within this context – as a non-essential item, laboriously transported over thousands of miles, it re-asserts the scale and depth of the imported lifestyle early missionaries sought to establish. In the isolation of the Khwebe Hills, the familiarity of household items and games such as chess would no doubt have brought comfort and reassurance to the new inhabitants. However, beyond this, the presence of a chess set offered a material and cerebral link to a world of rationalism and logic. Whether Wookey taught others the game, or played as a source of personal entertainment, the chess pawn nevertheless presented a material proxy for, and avenue to, ordered, logical thought.

Despite the recovery of this cornucopia of personal goods and household comestibles, it is clear that it was still a daily challenge to survive. The local environment was not conducive to self-sufficiency – wild animals attacked stock and locusts decimated fledgling attempts at agriculture.[39] One member of the mission, John Reid, was sent back to Britain after being crippled by a leopard attack in 1895.[40] Reporting in the Annual Report of the LMS for 1896, Wookey states:

> *The life of a missionary on the Kgwebe Hills may have its romantic side, but it requires faith and courage, and persistence of a very high order to continue this work.*[41]

For all their wealth in European materiality, Wookey and associates were physically incapable of weathering the harsh realities of the Khwebe Hills, let alone taming or transforming them. The archaeology provides a final twist – the very recovery of such an object and its associated material wealth demands scrutiny. How and why was this chess piece left at the mission? The answer lies in the final days of the Lake Ngami mission: Wookey left for Palapye in 1895, intent on regrouping, amassing much needed supplies, and returning to the Khwebe Hills. However, repeated malarial attacks denied him such redemption and he was forced to return to Britain in May 1897 to convalesce, never to return to the Khwebe

39 CWM/LMS/S Africa/Incoming Correspondence/1894/Box 51/Folder 2/Jacket C/5070.
40 CWM/LMS/S Africa/Incoming Correspondence/1895/Box 52/Folder 1/Jacket C/5646.
41 Report of the Directors to the General Meeting of the Missionary Society 1896, 150 (LMS 1896).

Hills.[42] The Lake Ngami mission was abandoned, and the buildings and material remains left to the elements. Thus, the archaeology, and particularly the lonely chess piece, simultaneously represents both the materialisation of an intellectual ideal, as well as the ultimate failure and collapse of that particular venture.

42 CWM/LMS/S Africa/Incoming Correspondence/1897/Box 54/Folder 1/Jacket C/7778.

EFATE NEW HEBRIDES
KO MROA KI AU

Communion Tokens, Vanuatu

Eve Haddow

This metal disc once granted its bearer permission to celebrate Holy Communion, one of the important ritual occasions in the life of a practising Christian. As suggested by its inscription, it is a communion token associated with the island of Efate in Vanuatu, previously the New Hebrides. The reverse reads "*Ko mroa ki au*", which in the Efate language means "Think on me". It is part of the D. L. Edwards communion token collection held by Perth Museum and Art Gallery in Scotland. Produced around 1903 with many others in its likeness, the origins of this particular sacramental ticket can be traced back to 16th century Scotland.

The use of tokens as a means to identify those who have been properly instructed and admitted to the Lord's Supper is often attributed to Calvin in 16th century Geneva (MacMillan 1999, ii). Token usage quickly spread to other European countries. Their development in Scotland is interwoven with the emerging Presbyterian Church and the Reformation of 1560, although they are recorded as being used before the official date of the Reformation and some even believe they originated in the Roman *medalli* issued for Catholic Mass (Burnet 1960, 62). Tokens were usually metal, but occasionally fashioned of wood. They were presented to baptised individuals by church elders to indicate permission to take Communion. The frequency of Communion for Presbyterians varies but has always been much less than in the Catholic Church or the Church of England, and even today may only occur two to four times a year. A candidate for Communion was expected to be both a practising Christian and educated in the scriptures, the latter being tested through catechism.

During the complex events of the period from the Reformation to 1690, when the Scottish Presbyterian church emerged as the institution it was in the 18th and 19th centuries, communion tokens held significance for Covenanters. Many restrictions were placed on Presbyterians but some Ministers rejected from the church continued to hold secret outdoor Communions. Tokens enabled them to distinguish friend from foe (Burnet 1960, 149). Metal tokens were in common usage until the late 19th century. They were gradually replaced by cards, although some churches used tokens into the 20th century. While not uniquely Scottish, nor restricted to practising Presbyterians, it is certain that Communion tokens

Figure 1. Communion token from Efate, Vanuatu, produced 1903. Part of the D. L. Edwards collection of communion tokens, Perth Museum & Art Gallery, 28/1935. Photograph courtesy of Perth Museum & Art Gallery, Perth & Kinross Council, Scotland.

were particularly favoured in Scotland and had a significant role in the country's Reformed religious life. They became intricately bound with Scottish Presbyterian practice and, as Scots began to settle in other parts of the world, tokens travelled with them.

The first communion token to arrive in Vanuatu actually made its journey there via Canada. This is materially evident in the oval token's inscription, reading, "Parish of Pictou", and on the reverse, "Rev'd T. McC. 1810". Thomas McCulloch was a minister in Pictou, Nova Scotia from 1804 to 1843 (Burzinski 1999, 301). Aberdeenshire-born missionary Reverend John Geddie, who emigrated to Pictou as a young boy, then took a set of these tokens to Vanuatu in 1848. He settled at Anelgauhat on the southwest of the island of Aneityum. His travelling companion, Reverend Powell of the London Missionary Society, only remained there a year. In 1852, Geddie fully established Aneityum's first Christian church with the baptism of fifteen local people and the celebration of Communion with these new members (Patterson 1882, 323). This was the first Presbyterian Communion in Vanuatu into which newly converted Christians of Vanuatu were admitted. After the challenging experiences of early missionaries in the area, Geddie's work was highly significant for the Presbyterian Church.

A second metal Communion token of rectangular shape with cut corners is also associated with Aneityum. Its inscription reads, "*Aco Nedo Ineicki Par Imiehva Nyak, I Kor. XI. 24*", which translates from the Aneityum language to "do this in remembrance of me". The reference to the verse of Corinthians from which it comes is commonly represented on Scottish Presbyterian tokens. The reverse reads, "*Nakalasia, Aneiteum, 1852*", "*Nakalasia*" being the Aneityum word for "Christian". The year may refer to the first admission of church members. The most recent token from Vanuatu, on which this essay is based, is associated with Reverend J. W. MacKenzie, stationed in Erakor on Efate from 1872–1912. It provided a replacement for the initial Pictou token (Burzinski 1999, 301).

The inscriptions on these Communion tokens connect them to Efate and Aneityum. In the published accounts of missionaries stationed on other islands in Vanuatu, there are references to celebrating Communion but little mention of tokens (see Paton 1905; Paton 1911; Leggatt 1896). Whether this is because tokens were not used on other islands or because they were so bound up in the ritual of Communion that they escaped comment is uncertain. An account of tokens was written by Reverend Robert Steel, a minister from Sydney who toured Vanuatu on a mission vessel in 1874. A Communion season at Anelgauhat, Aneityum was regularly held to coincide with the annual gathering of Presbyterian missionaries at the Mission Synod. In describing the distribution of tokens on Friday 12 June prior to the Communion service on Sunday, Steel (1880, 373) writes:

> *It was rather striking to see the old Scottish custom of pewter tokens at a communion season in the South Sea Islands. Even in Australia there are few congregations that use them. But the missionaries on Aneityum are Presbyterians, and though the people know nothing of the name, and are Christians only, their spiritual guides have led them into the practices that are quite characteristic of Scotland.*

Around two hundred people from the island celebrated Communion, with people travelling from inland especially to attend the central church.

It is unclear when Communion token use ceased in Vanuatu. The original tokens brought from Pictou were reportedly sent back to Nova Scotia after being replaced (Burzinski 1999, 301). Reverend James Hay Lawrie of Edinburgh, a missionary on Aneityum from 1879 to 1896, donated two of the 1852 Aneityum tokens to the National Museum of Scotland in 1898, which may suggest those particular tokens were falling out of use by that time. Given the significance of sacramental tickets, it seems unlikely Lawrie would have brought them home if still being circulated. Of course, Lawrie and his wife may have kept the tokens as personal mementoes. A number of Vanuatu tokens are preserved in public and private collections, providing a material reminder of relationships of contact and exchange, but what of the many others produced? In Scotland, old tokens were often melted down in the past so the metal could be reused, or were buried under the church pulpit and forgotten (Burnet 1960, 198). Could this interment have happened in Vanuatu? Current excavation work by the Department of Archaeology at Australian National University, focusing on mission sites in southern Vanuatu, has yet to uncover any Communion tokens but they remain an artefact of interest in ongoing research.

Photograph, Democratic Republic of Congo

Jocelyne Dudding

This intimate moment between mother and daughter, preserved by the camera of the missionary Reverend Kenred Smith, resonates with images of the Madonna of Humility with the Child Jesus in her lap. As with other devotional imagery, the beauty and status of the two is emphasised by the iconography; the tribal marks on the mother's face and her heavy ostrich shell neck ornaments; the head binding of the child and her string of waist beads to protect her from evil spirits. Although likely to have been posed, the mother appears comfortable in front of the camera – the informality of the moment is further emphasised by the young boy sneaking into the frame in the background. What is unclear is whether Smith is unconsciously responding to widespread mother and child imagery or deliberately referencing Madonna and Child depictions. Smith, and the Baptist Mission in Congo, certainly used religious iconography in their teaching, as can be seen in a photograph of the interior of the Yakusu School-Chapel, where Smith served, which is abundantly decorated with prints depicting religious iconography (published in Herbert Sutton Smith 1911, 194). However, Madonna and Child representations are more closely associated with the Catholic Church than with the pared down iconography of the Baptist Church.

Rev. Smith took the photograph during his service for the Baptist Missionary Society in Congo between 1896 and 1914. Smith was a Cambridgeshire man but trained at the Baptist College at Bristol. Following in the footsteps of an illustrious former student, George Grenfell, who established the Baptist Mission in Congo in 1878, Smith's first posting in 1895 was to the newly established missionary station at Upoto, on the Upper Congo River (BMS World Mission n.d., 353-4). His missionary responsibilities involved extensive travel through the vast district, primarily along the upper stretches of the river via the mission steamer. Smith is known for his work translating the scriptures into Niger Kordofanian languages and his monthly contributions to *Wonderlands – The Young Folk's Magazine of the Baptist Missionary Society*; less well known are his 252 ethnographic photographs held at the Museum of Archaeology and Anthropology (MAA) in Cambridge.

Figure 1. "Bapoto. Woman suckling child, N. Congo. Child's head bound. Woman wearing ostrich-shell bead necklace." Photograph by Rev. Kenred Smith, c.1905. Museum of Archaeology and Anthropology, University of Cambridge. N.35273.VH.

The first set of seven photographs by Smith was accessioned by MAA in 1904 after John E. Foster, Secretary of the Cambridge Antiquarian Society, sent them to Baron von Hügel, MAA's first curator, on 13 November, writing:

> *I hope you consider the accompanying photos of Congo taken by a missionary at Bopoto good enough for the Museum. Is there any special information you want about them?*[43]

Von Hügel was obviously pleased, responding:

> *What an interesting set of Congo photographs. I have made a selection. I think one or two of the photos have been touched up or cut smaller (? For decency's sake). It would be wise for anthropological purposes to have them as taken if possible.*[44]

Only one photograph of these first seven survives (MAA 1904.163), showing "Women carrying loads". Comparing it to the subsequently acquired glass plate negative makes it clear that it has been cropped to a square format, with the result that only three women remain on the glass plate as compared to four on the original. Why is less obvious. The corner on the plate has been broken after this print was made, and even though the woman cropped from the image is clearly pregnant, von Hügel's proposition about "decency" appears unlikely given the other women's lack of dress. Smith may have cropped the right side of the negative with its background clutter of the man and hut to simplify the image, but in doing so he made the mission setting of the photograph less apparent, effectively excluding the signs of modernity and European influence.

In December 1904, Foster forwarded a further seventy-three of Smith's prints to von Hügel,[45] in response to which he enthused that these "'*will do*' for me!"[46]

> *I have written enclosed letter with a view to your perhaps being able to perhaps forward it to Rev. Smith. I did not like to say anything as to our desires in the line of objects, but as you know we have practically nothing from those regions & in spite of the scanty attire of the people, the sights of these photographs, makes me long to pull the little they wear off & so fill our cases!*[47]

The letter found its way to Kenred Smith, who replied via his two brothers in February 1905. Oswin Smith, who lived in Cambridge, wrote that a fellow missionary had just returned from the Congo and delivered to his "photographic brother" ninety negatives from Kenred, "some of which he thinks would suit you admirably".[48] Kenred's "photographic brother" was Harold Smith, a partner in Pearce & Smith Photographic Studio, Stanford Hill, London. Harold developed and printed Kenred's negatives, and possibly also supplied him with equipment and photographic instruction.

---

43 MAA Archives, Foster, 6.12.1904.
44 MAA Archives, von Hügel, 6.12.1905.
45 MAA Archives, Foster, 13.11.1904.
46 MAA Archives, von Hügel, 4.2.1905, von Hügel's emphasis.
47 MAA Archives, von Hügel, 4.2.1905, second letter.
48 MAA Archives, Smith, Oswin, 17.2.1905.

Von Hügel made clear the sorts of images he desired in a response to a third set of prints, on 27 May 1905:

> *Some are of considerable interest to us, but the majority are not serviceable for our purposes as the natives are dressed in European cloth, &c, &c. As you know I want to show their characteristic, physical development or modification of the body – scars &c, or their occupations.*[49]

In December 1905, von Hügel supplemented this note by sending Kenred a copy of *Anthropological Notes & Queries* (Garson and Read 1899),[50] which Kenred considered would "assist me in the future in securing some ethnographical information of real interest".[51] Despite repeated requests for photographs of physical types, "of the same individual taken full front view, back, and from the two sides in profile, so as to show the whole figure with all scars, etc.",[52] Kenred did not provide von Hügel with any such anthropometric imagery. His reluctance to photograph newly converted Christians without their clothes perhaps expressed a reluctance to undo the work of clothing them, but possibly more significantly, a concern with betraying the trust of those on whom he relied in his daily work.

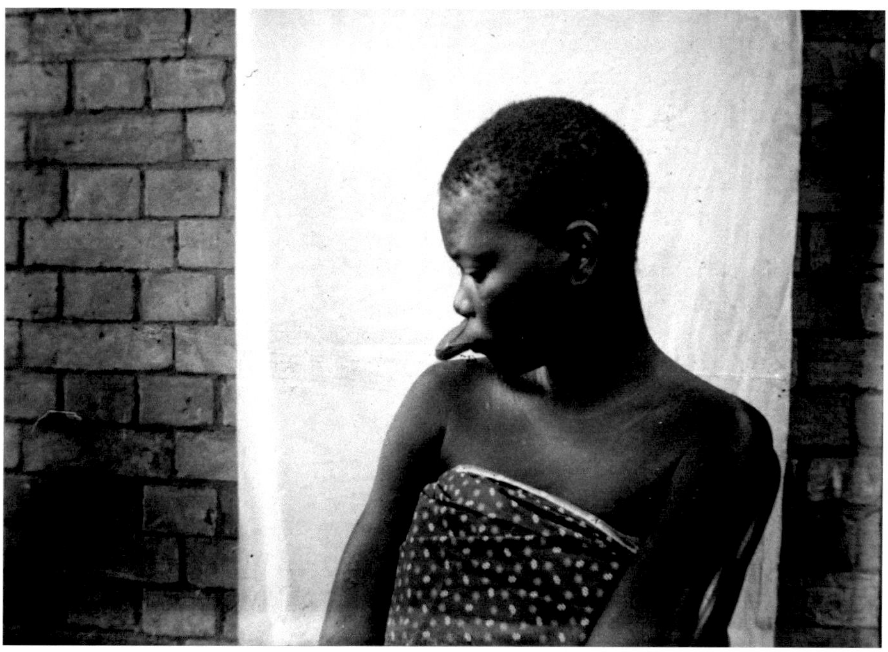

Figure 2. "Woman with distended lip for ornament. N. Congo. Basoko." Photograph by Kenred Smith, c.1905–1914, reprinted by Alfred Haddon, c.1935. Cambridge Museum of Archaeology and Anthropology, P.7201.ACH1.

49 MAA Archives, von Hügel, 27.6.1905.

50 MAA Archives, von Hügel, 9.12.1905.

51 MAA Archives, Smith, Kenred, 6.12.1905.

52 MAA Archives, von Hügel 8.4, 1905. Also see 4.2.1905, 27.6.1905, 23.3.1906.

Von Hügel's response was to either crop evidence of Western influence from Smith's photographs, or to reject such images entirely, even when they provided the anthropometrical information he sought, such as in a photograph of a woman wearing a lip plug (Figure 2). Nevertheless, von Hügel's Cambridge colleague Alfred Cort Haddon used this same image in his Mounted Print Collection for teaching anthropology at the University. Smith himself also published a similar portrait of the same woman, which he captioned "The Decorations of Her Tribe" in his *Congoland: A Book for Young People* (Smith 1920, 50).

In contrast to what von Hügel may have desired, many of Smith's portraits feature individuals who appear aware of the camera and able to respond to it in a fairly self-conscious manner. For example, in the photograph of the women suckling her child, it is unclear whether she dressed for the camera, or whether her neck ornament is everyday wear. When considering that Margaret Carey (1986, 9) suggests that it would constitute a full day's work to chip, bore and grind one hundred ostrich eggshell beads, and that each strand of the neck ornament consists of over four hundred beads, a sense may be gained of the time taken to create the ornament, its likely exchange value, and therefore the likely significance of being photographed wearing it. Similarly, Smith's group portraits suggest the deployment of the camera by Congolese people to record their own relationships between both people and their spaces (see Lydon 2005, 72). This, combined with the number of "occupation" photographs showing people involved in everyday and social activities, suggests that Smith's photographs may be more valuable for Congolese people today as an example of their cultural heritage than they ever were for von Hügel as anthropological images.

"Bowl", Solomon Islands

Nick Stanley

Gallery 33, "A Meeting Ground of Cultures", opened in 1990 at Birmingham Museum, providing Birmingham's ethnographic collections with a permanent display location for the first time in decades. The gallery was organised along thematic lines and one of its cases was devoted to eating and drinking. Within this case is an object that has been there for the last quarter-century. Its current label states that is a "Christian Communion Cup, Solomon Islands, 1912–1922" and notes that it was made using traditional techniques and materials, such as coconut inlaid with shell. Linking to the overarching themes of the case, it goes on to claim that "it was made for the consumption of wine at the heart of the Christian ceremony of communion" and concludes with the information that it was collected by Edith Sunderland.

Edith Sunderland was a member of the Melanesian Mission who worked at St Hilda's Girls' School between 1922 and 1923 on the island of Bunana, near Small Gela in the central Solomon Islands. She gave her collection to Birmingham Museum in 1978, over fifty years after her time in the Solomon Islands, when the object in question was labelled and registered as a bowl. The term "bowl" hardly seems to fit – it is much more like a cup – so, how did it become misidentified in the accessions register? The cataloguer probably had little knowledge of the original context in which it was made and was simply stumped for a better description. Its current description as a Communion cup appears more satisfactory, but is this new description really that much better than its predecessor? The object lacks some of the major features one would expect to see in a communion cup or chalice. Firstly, the materials are unusual. The cup itself is not made of metal but rather of coconut shell, with an inlay of local mother of pearl. It is the overall shape of the object that conforms more closely to our expectations of a Communion cup. The shape and decoration combine two sets of expectations in what I have elsewhere described as a syncretic object (Stanley 1989, 94). By this I mean that it combines features of a Western Communion cup with a form of manufacture specific to the Solomon Islands. In particular, the incised shell decoration as a decorative form has become a stylistic signature, widely identified with the region.

Figure 1. Edith Sunderland's "bowl", Birmingham Museum, 1978A4. Courtesy and Copyright, Birmingham Museums Trust.

Figure 2. Melanesian Court, Hamilton Exhibition, June 1932. Kinder Library Album 6, Anglican Board of Missions series 9, p. 23. With permission from the Provincial Archives Committee, St. John's College Library, Auckland.

Di Smith (2010, 201) has recently suggested that the continual exchange of gifts between teachers and students at the missionary school on Bunana was a regular feature of their interaction, making for reciprocal and egalitarian relationships rather than "a culture engulfed by missionary ideals". But to participate fully in school life, the girls had to make regular offerings during church services. Since they had no money, the missionaries hit upon a novel system, "make and earn". Ida Wench (1961, 185), the senior teacher at the school, wrote:

> *I suppose we could have provided the girls with money for the offertory, but we felt that to have done so would not have taught them the spirit and nature of giving. Then we hit on a system that had much to commend it. We invited them to manufacture useful articles, such as brooms, coco-nut leaf mats and loosely woven bags, which we promised to buy from them.*

Wench (1961, 185) also noted that "the San Cristovalites became particularly adept at manufacturing cups from coconut shells". It is possible that girls arriving at the school from the eastern Solomon Islands had the necessary craft skills and may have made the Communion cup as part of the "make and earn" programme. But there are two reasons to question whether they did indeed do so. First, the Communion cup does not fit into the egalitarian and reciprocal relationship between students and teachers described by Smith, involving gifts of necklaces, armlets, dancing ornaments, spoons and money. Spoons come nearest as they too were made from coconut shell, but are far more everyday objects. Communion cups are traditionally associated with male priests, and the school was a wholly female environment. Second, there is a question as to whether the San Cristovalites

Figure 3. Altar cross, Birmingham Museum & Art Gallery, on loan from the Melanesian Mission, 1992W13. Courtesy and Copyright, Birmingham Museums Trust.

had the necessary skills to complete the inlay, as although Wench mentions coconut shell cups, she does not specify that these involved inlay. Tridacna shell inlay was traditionally associated with canoes (especially the *nguzu-nguzu* prow figures) and feast bowls, but was later extended into the decoration of crosses and altars by Christian Makira craftsmen. Is it possible that the Communion cup was not made on Bunana by schoolgirls, but rather by a more mature hand in a different place? In which case, how did it come to be in Edith Sunderland's collection?

Although Edith Sunderland was in the Solomon Islands in 1922–1923, it is possible that she could have acquired the Communion cup elsewhere, perhaps from a missionary source in England during the period before her collection arrived at Birmingham Museum in 1978. Missionaries regularly gave and sold items when home on furlough (Stanley 1994, 36). Objects sent from the missions became emblematic of the missionary field and were regularly displayed to promote missionary fundraising. All the major missionary societies held exhibitions as a significant promotional activity, but these also served as fundraising events. Such objects were regularly solicited by the organisers of missionary exhibitions, and Edith Sunderland undoubtedly would have been called on to contribute to such events.

Many objects in the exhibition were for sale, and a photograph from the Hamilton Exhibition in 1932 (Figure 2) shows strings of bags displayed with a price tag of 2/- and 3/- apiece. Melanesian Courts were very popular and as the

New Zealand Herald noted in relation to another similar exhibition, 'Without making any invidiuos distinctions, the Melanesian Court may be said to be the outstanding feature of the exhibition' and noted there are wood carvings and shell ornaments, some the product of the pre-missionary era and some the product of native schools conducted by the European and native teachers' (Ross 1983, 66). While we can reject the possibility that Edith Sunderland's Communion cup is of pre-missionary provenance, it is less easy to dismiss the possibility of it having been made by a teacher or craftsperson in the Makira district. In which case, what was it made for? It is extremely unlikely that such Communion cups would have been used for church ritual purposes. It should be seen, perhaps, rather more like the inlaid crosses also made in the Solomon Islands – an example of which is just visible in the photograph at the centre of the Melanesian Court – as a universally recognisable religious symbol incorporating local decorative features. The Church of Melanesia has regularly employed such decoration throughout its churches as a way of acknowledging indigenous influence on its modes of introduced Christian practice (Figure 3).

Whether purchased by Sunderland at a missionary exhibition, given to her in England by a visiting missionary or acquired from the girls at Bunana, the communion cup serves for us as a poignant historical reminder of an early episode in the evangelisation of the Solomon Islands, and demonstrates just how important female involvement was in that venture. It is striking that it may equally have served as a poignant personal reminder for Sunderland herself. It is surely significant that all of the three missionaries working together on the island in 1923 (Ida Wench, Edith Sunderland and Edith Safstrom) sent collections home. Each used objects from their collections to enliven accounts of their missionary work abroad, and, when they no longer fulfilled this function, gave their collections a new life in their local museums: Birmingham (Wench and Sunderland) and Melbourne (Safstrom).

How should we regard the object that remains on display in the museum at Birmingham today? It is very difficult to determine its provenance. It can clearly no longer be consigned to the ambiguous description of "bowl", and may only very loosely be considered a Communion cup, since it is unlikely to have ever been used as one. It is tempting to assign it to the enthusiasm of the missionary school girls, engaging in new skills and activities that were traditionally male. If, as the teachers observed, the girls from the different islands taught each other these skills, this raises interesting questions about the forms of influence and diffusion that arose from the encounters made possible by missionary activity.

Whoever made it, the object in question remains a curious talisman of the missionary endeavour, whilst simultaneously embodying forms of decoration that are heavily inflected with the tradition of the prow heads and large decorated bowls from the Makira district. Whether it was made by the industrious girls at St. Hilda's school through a "make and earn" scheme, or by older and probably male craftsmen on their home islands, it is clearly a "syncretic object" and remains a "curio", to use the terminology of its own time.

Parade knife, Democratic Republic of Congo

Johanna Zetterstrom-Sharp

In the summer of 1970, Rev. Lionel G. West was interviewed by David Boston, the then director of the Horniman Museum and Gardens, about a collection of "Congo curios" he had recently donated. The notes from the meeting suggest that during thirty-one years of missionary service for the Baptist Missionary Society (BMS), West had developed a deep interest in local cosmologies and beliefs in the north-western Belgian Congo. The collection, amassed between 1930 and 1961, largely comprises an assemblage of "fetishes" and "charms". It is well documented through West's own words, describing, for example, how a Mpama "fetish axe" is "used by women troubled by bad spirits", and a copper alloy coil is used to "protect against lightning". Perhaps the most curious of West's "curios" is an anthropomorphic parade knife, apparently "made locally for Mr West". With one arm raised in what appears to be a salute, and potentially constructed from parts with a much longer history, this object and its biography seem resonant with the changes and tensions which swept the Belgian Congo during these later years of colonial occupation.

Rev. Lionel West was posted to Lukolela, a small missionary station along the Congo River, ninety miles upstream from Bolobo. This area has a history of established Baptist missionary activity, with almost fifty years of continuity prior to West's arrival in 1933. In 1884, George Grenfell began to re-trace Henry Morton Stanley's earlier expedition, founding a series of stations for the BMS, beginning with Lukolela in 1885. West is likely to have arrived to find an existing congregation and support network, as well as local familiarity with the presence of foreign missionaries. West's obituary (BMS World Mission 1986) refers to him as "Ebaka", a name acquired in Lukolela which echoes "Ibaka", the principal chief of Bolobo at the arrival of the BMS in the 1880s (Johnston 1908, 389). It also notes that West became fluent in Lingala, which had begun to replace Bobangi as the primary spoken language, a likely result of Lingala being widely used in mission schools, Bible translations and hymns.

Figure 1. Anthropomorphic Knife collected by Rev. Lionel G. West in Lukolela, Équateur District, DR Congo. Horniman Museum and Gardens, 1970.33.

It is unclear how West amassed his collection of curios, but the focus on fetishes and charms would suggest that he sought them out, potentially in reaction to a rising need to record the practices which his institution aspired to change. He also appears to have had an eye for objects already popular in European institutions, including a magnificent Kuba *Ngaady aMwaash* mask and a polychrome Kuyu *Kebe Kebe* staff. As an object lacking in any contextual information, the anthropomorphic knife seems to ally more with this latter category. It bears a resemblance to the abundance of "fancy parade knives" in European collections, popular as souvenirs for colonial personnel and missionaries working in the region prior to independence in 1960 (Gosseau 1997, 58). The form of this body of weaponry derives from a group of knives allegedly used for ritual beheadings, the role of which is said to have changed at the turn of the nineteenth century due in part to pressures from missionaries and King Leopold II's administration to bring an end to human sacrifice (Johnston 1908, 384-407). Increasingly valued as symbols of prestige, more elaborate designs were implemented as their functionality as cutting blades became less important.

Despite the abundance of Congolese parade knives, anthropomorphic knives such as this are rare. It is unclear whether West commissioned the knife himself, playing an active role in its form, or whether it was crafted by someone independently with the intention of selling or giving it to him. Gosseau (1997, 58) suggests that similar knives may have emerged in response to "ideas probably suggested to people of this region by Europeans". They show clear resemblance to the double sickle knives collected along the Congo River, particularly the Lobala, Ngbaka and Bondjo weapons, which Gosseau (1997, 44) notes were often compared by European visitors to human forms. The relative scarcity of comparable examples suggests that West's knife is likely to have been the product of an individual's imagination rather than one of an established form, whether that be under West's direction, the blacksmith's own initiative, or indeed a combination of both.

The knife itself appears as though it may have been constructed as a composite of older objects. Its wooden handle has a deep patina and worn edges, suggesting that it has been heavily handled. The "blade" bears shallow indentations along its shaft, as though an older motif has been hammered out and then filed, and the figure's long neck looks as though it has been coarsely soldered on. Could this be the recycling of an older knife no longer valued, modified with the intention of making it more appealing to foreign curiosity? The knife is quite roughly made, inserted at a slight angle into the hilt, and whilst other examples of parade knives are often uniformly polished to a shine, this example looks unfinished. It seems unlikely that it would have been made with the intention of parading, supporting the idea that it was indeed "made for" West.

Its form poses further questions. One arm is raised toward the head at a forty-five degree angle, as if in salute, whilst the other hangs straight by its side; the figure also appears to be wearing a cap. It is difficult to ignore the evocation of a soldier; certainly the area had a history of tense contact with King Leopold II's Free State Force Publique. The area was taken over by the Belgian government in 1908 due to its proximity to trade posts along the tributaries of the Congo River. It is also interesting to consider whether activities associated with the Belgian Congo's allegiance to the Allied Forces during World War II may be of significance. It would appear that Belgian Congo forces amassed in former Léopoldville (now Kinshasa) and advanced up the Congo River in 1941, passing Lukolela on route to the Abyssinian front at Saio as part of the British East African Campaign (Ready 1985, 45). One might expect that such an event would have proved significant for West and his congregation, due to the prevalence of the British-based BMS stations in the region, the huge expansion of the military during the period, and the implications of this for the violence that led to independence in 1960 and West's subsequent departure.

This curious knife, presented to David Boston in 1970, may once have been read as an indication of the Congo as a strange and undeniably different place; a place in need of transformation through Western intervention such as missionary work. It appears, however, to rather encapsulate the very process of transformation, with new gods, languages and leaders inscribed into its very fabric. It speaks of the complexity and tensions at the heart of the colonial encounter in the former Belgian Congo, resonating with the successful establishment of a new religion on the one hand, and the centrality of military force on the other.

Evangelika Presbiteria Hame

KELILI ƉASEƉIGBALẼ

Ŋkɔ Gladys Renate Abena Adobor

Exɔ Mawutsi le HO Ŋkeke 1963

Fofo Theodore K. Adobor Dada Victoria Adobor

Exɔ Kelili le TAMALE Ŋkeke 28/8/77

Yayranya Kpɔ ɖa, megbɔna kaba; lé nusi le asiwò me la, ɖe asi sesie, bena amea ɖeke nagaxɔ wò Fiakuku la o.

Nyaɖeɖefia 3"

Nutome KUMASI

Osɔfo G.A. Gbedi

E.P. CHURCH PRESS, HO

Interview

Atta Kwami and Chris Wingfield

Atta Kwami is a painter, printmaker, independent art historian and curator whose work explores the dynamism, rhythmic structures and the power of improvisation in African visual practices. He trained and taught in Kumasi, Ghana and the UK. His work can be found in major collections including the National Museums of Ghana and Kenya; the National Museum of African Art, Washington, DC; the Metropolitan Museum of Art, New York, and the British Museum. He was a Visiting Fellow at the Cambridge/Africa Collaborative Research Programme on Art and Museums in Africa, 2012-13, as part of which he visited Ghana with Wingfield for a final project workshop.

CW: I understand that your own family's history has a strong involvement with missionaries and missionary history in Ghana.

AK: Yes, there was a strong involvement with the Church on both my mother and father's side. My great-grandfather, Stefano Kwami, was captured and enslaved as a young man by Muslim traders in the north and taken south to the coast, to Keta in the Volta Region of Ghana. Missionaries from the North German (Bremen) Missionary Society were active there in the nineteenth century and paid to free my great-grandfather. He was named after the town in Germany that contributed the money to buy his freedom. As Stefano was freed on a Saturday, he took Kwami (Saturday-born) as his surname.

CW: So were the missionaries quite involved with the history of slavery in Ghana?

AK: Well, up to a point. Some of the early fieldworkers for the mission, like my great-grandfather, had been slaves. They went around as catechists, singing the gospel into the hearts of people, to get them converted to Christianity. My great-grandfather married in the Volta region and his son, Robert Stephen Kwami (1879–1945), was taken to Germany at the age of fifteen to be educated by the mission. After he returned in 1911, he was ordained and became a pastor for the church, working in various places. He became well-known for his social work and sermons.

Figure 1. Baptismal certificate of the Evangelical Presbyterian Church, dove design by Grace Salome Kwami. Photograph by Atta Kwami, 2014.

CW: It is interesting that in Europe when people think of missionaries they often think of the European missionaries, but much of the spread of Christianity in Africa was down to Africans.

AK: That's true. It became a point of debate later in assessing the role of missionaries and the approaches they adopted. If things had been left in the hands of the Africans, things might have taken a different form. There was probably too much control on the part of the German missionaries to begin with. Water finds its own level, and the requirements of the community might have been a better guide for building the church. In 1917, during the First World War, when the German Missionaries were expelled, my grandfather, Robert Stephen Kwami, led a movement that agitated for the establishment of an Ewe Protestant church that would be independent from the German Bremen Missionary Society – so you see how convoluted and complex these stories are, deciding on such an important matter in accordance with African custom, with the involvement of Christians and non-Christians. From 1922 until his death in 1945, he was the Synod Clerk. On my mother's side there were also people who worked as evangelists and as teachers.

CW: Do you think that education and literacy was an important part of the mission and the church for many people?

AK: It was. My maternal grandfather, Rev. Theodor Kwami Anku, and his son Victor Oscar Anku, built a school at Gbadzeme in the Volta region, which was a huge effort. My grandfather was the headteacher and my mother, the artist Grace Salome Kwami, also trained as a teacher before later going to art school.

CW: I believe your mother also worked for some German missionaries as a young woman?

AK: She was employed as a housemaid and was learning to cook for the missionaries at Amedzofe. There was an anecdote she liked to recount about when she was baking for them one day and burnt the bread. The missionaries became quite angry and said, "We come here, and we sacrifice so much to help you people, and you burn our bread!" [Laughs…]

CW: The fact that she liked to tell that story says quite a lot.

AK: They didn't realize that she was so young, and they later apologized that they were working her so hard. The Germans had a system of "*Hauskinder*", where they took on children as part of the household. She knew a few German songs, and occasionally burst into song.

CW: Do you think that experience had an impact on her later artistic work?

AK: She carried on dressmaking and crocheting, which she took to great heights and adapted to local needs, making things like hunter's hats. One of the objects that I remember from this whole missionary encounter was a volume of German wood engravings that my mother had, which belonged to my maternal grandfather.

Figure 2. Greeting card by Grace Salome Kwami, showing mother and child. Photograph by Atta Kwami, 2014.

It included depictions of stories from the Bible. My mother used this book as a reference, and explored new forms of representation, mostly the Holy Trinity or Madonna and Child, not only in drawings and sketches but also in sculptures.

CW: Was the pictorial imagery of Christianity significant for many people?

AK: Yes, the use of images was much more restrained than in the Catholic Church, but the walls of many village chapels and churches showed depictions of Christ, the Ten Commandments and other passages from the Bible. It was a form of visual literacy that was very direct and made an impact.

CW: I know that your mother explored traditional African religious practices in her later life, but for someone of her generation growing up, would she have been more at home with the church?

AK: It's very complex. Although her mother became Christian and was married to a minister, she knew about traditional African religion and practices, so they were rounded in their belief systems. They knew about the shrines and priests, and in a lot of her narrations of her life she described certain experiences in ways that suggested there was a mainstream, and then this new religion which changed their lives in a modern sense. Her illustration for a newspaper article on "Religions of the

Figure 3. Artist Book, Grace Kwami Sculpture (1993) by Atta Kwami. Paper, millboard, cloth.
Photograph by Franko Khoury, National Museum of African Art, Smithsonian Institution.

World" (now lost) engaged with pluralism in various forms of worship in the then Gold Coast. Nonetheless, the newspaper cutting I saw as a child may be considered a bridge between the past and the present; the colony and the post-colony.

CW: We are exploring the idea of the curio as something that was created, which can't be explained by established practices in either Africa or Europe – a creative blending by people who had a foot in each world. I was thinking about your artist book, *Grace Kwami Sculpture*, as something that might be regarded as a curio or curiosity in this sense?

AK: It's great you mentioned this because I didn't know how to introduce it. It is a book created in the form of a spider. In Ghana, the spider figure Kweku Ananse denotes ingenuity and skill. It has eight legs and you can make an entry anywhere into the story of Grace Kwami that I have assembled. I made this book in 1993, but the gestation period was probably ten years.

CW: I can see a number of mother and child figures and the figures are clearly African, but are they an interpretation of Christian imagery?

AK: I think so. There are quite a lot of mother and child images, but also women preparing meals and carrying out household chores. The whole process of change from biblical illustrations into groups and portraits originates from that encounter with Western forms of depiction. But my mother also took from local ways of working and was curious to find out what was going on around her. The Church was keen to encourage this in later years, when it was well established. It became an important source of patronage for many African artists, including for my mother, who was asked to design baptismal certificates, greeting cards and a special cloth to celebrate one hundred years of the church in Ghana.

CW: Is that bird on the sculpture a Christian dove figure?

AK: Yes, it features in a lot of the Christian literature, but on its left we also have the *Sankofa* bird, a bird with its head turning backwards. It is associated with the proverb that there is nothing wrong with learning from the past. That became the guiding principle for many Ghanaian modern artists in the 1960s, after the overthrow of Kwame Nkrumah. Before then, his notion of the "African Personality" was guiding them into the modern age.

CW: So your sculpture brings in the importance of Ananse the spider, but the book form also links to literacy, education, and the significance of the Bible as a book.

AK: I am interested in artists' books and have made a few, but I remember in 1965 at Sunday school in Ho we had a Dutch teacher who set us a contest – we had read about the story of St Paul and were talking about scrolls, so we were asked to make scrolls. I made a scroll with wooden handles and decorated it with beads with help from my mother. Incidentally, it won the prize, which was another book, a book about St Paul, which I still have among my treasures. This connection between literacy, learning and the book, and me making my first artist's book – which actually didn't have anything written on the paper, so was a kind of conceptual artwork – the sense of volume, of being able to unscroll and roll it up again was fascinating for me. So now we have this, which is its own portable, moveable museum, in a sense.

CW: But it takes the form of a sort of book in a box?

AK: This point you make about the literacy and book form as a curio is profoundly felt in Ghana. Recently, when I had my book launch for *Kumasi Realism* (Kwami 2013), I realized that many of my relatives were so supportive in buying copies and taking these away because the book is so important as a form of knowledge. Knowledge is seen as something almost close to scripture in the way that people handle it.

CW: Many missionary societies, particularly Protestant missionary societies, saw themselves as promoting the word, the Bible as a book, and many African languages were written down for the first time by missionaries creating bible translations.

AK: But it also seeps down to grassroots art and culture. There is a very famous Ewe proverb that says that the black thread is like the word, it does not refuse any cloth. So the image of black ink and black thread is woven into any kind of text or textile, and that I think is beautiful.

CW: I know that in Ghana today, Christianity is a very powerful force, but often through newer Pentecostal forms of Christianity. Does Ghana's missionary history inform this?

AK: The proliferation of churches is probably a new phenomenon which has come from these charismatic churches in the US, but because there has been a background of missionary involvement and churches, that paved the way for them to function. Christianity has also been a major force in maintaining stability, and prayer meetings for peace during elections are important. Many people who are not educated would expect to gain some education or literacy from the church and the government recognizes that this is an important backing role for them. But many churches are also a menace because they make so much noise within residential areas. I don't mind good singing but it is the fact that they use microphones and blare it out. But I should advocate the independence of these churches in the way that my grandfather did.

CW: Many scholars talk about conversion and particularly new forms of Christianity as a form of rupture, modernisation and separation from the past, but it seems like there was a refusal to make this rupture in the work of Grace Kwami.

AK: I think so. In a sense, honouring her memory by establishing a museum would celebrate and open up some of these ideas for discussion. Many of the churches in the south of Ghana have no archive or museum. The archives are largely in Europe, with a few counter-examples.

CW: Does the fact that there aren't archives or museum collections make people's sense of this past more shallow?

AK: There have been efforts to document and address the lack of literature through a number of books, but the classic book on the Ewe remains that by Jakob Spieth, a Bremen missionary/anthropologist, originally published in 1906 in German and Ewe. It has been referred to in court for confirming Ewe customs. The chiefs have forgotten many of the customs and ceremonies and are pleased to have this book republished in English, which it has been recently (Spieth 2011).

CW: But presumably many people like you will have family stories, like the story your mother told about burning the bread, which is so very evocative of a complex relationship, and captures something about the nature of that relationship.

AK: It does. But at the same time we can read into some of these narratives and see that there was more of a person-to-person and individual exchange.

CW: It is interesting that you have photographs of German missionaries mixed in within your family photographs.

AK: There were times when visiting Germans who were connected to the mission came to Ghana and they visited us. They would bring books and postcards with them. My father once drove to Germany from the UK to visit some German missionaries – he was also going to buy a Mercedes Benz to take back to Ghana.

References

Académie Tahitienne. 1999. *Dictionnaire Tahitien-Français. Fa'atoro Parau Tahiti-Farani.* Tahiti: Fare Fana'a, Tahiti.

Adams, R. 1998. *Framing the Native: Rev. James Hay Lawrie's photographs, 1891-1894.* Port Vila: Vanuatu National Museum.

Anderson, A. H. 2013. *To the Ends of the Earth: Pentecostalism and the Transformation of World Christianity.* Oxford: Oxford University Press.

Anonymous. 1889. "Museum of Science and Art: Specimens from the New Hebrides." *The Scotsman Newspaper* September 21, 1889, p. 7.

Arnold, K. 2006. *Cabinets for the Curious: Looking back at early English museums.* Aldershot: Ashgate.

Bagnoli, M., H. A. Klein and G. C. Mann (eds). 2010. *Treasures of Heaven: Saints, Relics, and Devotion in Medieval Europe.* London: British Museum Press.

Bell, J. A. 2013. "'Expressions of Kindly Feeling': The London Missionary Society Collections from the Papuan Gulf." In *Melanesia: Art and Encounter*, edited by L. Bolton, N. Thomas, L. Bonshek and J. Adams, 57-63. London: British Museum Press.

Beasley, H. G. 1928. *Pacific Island Records: Fish Hooks.* London: Seeley, Service & Co.

Blackbeard, M. 1985 "Memoirs of Samuel Blackbeard." *Botswana Notes and Records* 17: 187–91.

BMS World Mission. 1986. "Obituary for Rev. Lionel George West and Emily May West." In *1985/6 Baptist Handbook.* London: Baptist Missionary Society.

BMS World Mission. [n.d.]. "Memoirs of Ministers and Missionaries." Cited on napkin.net, [http://www.nap-kin.net/showsource.php?sourceID=S35&tree=napkin]. Accessed May 2014.

Bolton L. 2007. "Island Dress that Belongs to Us All." In *Body Arts and Modernity*, edited by E. Ewart and M. O'Hanlon, 165-82. Wantage: Sean Kingston Publishing.

Börjeson, L. and P. J. Lane. 1996. "Preliminary Archaeological Investigations at Phalatswe (Old Palapye), Central District, Botswana: The 1995 Season." *Nyame Akuma* 45: 2–10.

Bott, E. 1982. *Tongan Society at the Time of Captain Cook's Visits: Discussions with Her Majesty Queen Sālote Tupou.* Memoirs of the Polynesian Society 44. Wellington: The Polynesian Society.

Brewster, A. B. 1937. *King of the Cannibal Isles: A Tale of Early Life and Adventure in the Fiji Islands.* London: Robert Hale & Company.

Brown, G. 1908. *George Brown, D.D. Pioneer Missionary and Explorer: An Autobiography.* London: Hodder and Stoughton.

Burnet, G. B. 1960. *The Holy Communion in the Reformed Church of Scotland, 1560-1960.* Edinburgh: Oliver & Boyd.

Burt, B. 1991. "Inventory of the Melanesian Mission collection". London: British Museum.

Burt, B. 1994. *Tradition and Christianity: The Colonial Transformation of a Solomon Islands Society.* New York: Harwood Academic Publishers.

Burt, B. 2002. "The Story of Amasia: Whose History and Whose Epistemology?" *Journal of Pacific History* 37:187-204.

Burt, B. 2013. "Tracing Artefacts from the Melanesian Mission". In *Melanesia: Art and Encounter,* edited by L. Bolton, N. Thomas, E. Bonshek, J. Adams and B. Burt, 240-44. London: British Museum Press.

Burzinski, L. M. 1999. *Communion Tokens of the World.* Madison: Straus Printing Co.

Calvert, James. 1858. *Fiji and the Fijians. Volume II, Mission History.* Edited by G. S. Rowe. London: Heylin.

Campbell, I. C. 2001. *Island Kingdom: Tonga Ancient and Modern.* Christchurch: Canterbury University Press.

Campbell, J. 1815. *Travels in South Africa: Undertaken at the request of the Missionary Society.* London: Black and Parry.

Campbell, J. 1834. *Journal of Travels in South Africa; among the Hottentot and Other Tribes; in the Years 1812, 1813, and 1814.* London: Religious Tract Society.

Cannizzo, J. 1996. "Doctor Livingstone Collects." In *David Livingstone and the Victorian Encounter with Africa,* edited by J. M. MacKenzie, 141-65. London: National Portrait Gallery Publications.

Carey, M. 1986. *Beads and Beadwork of East and South Africa.* Michigan: Shire Publications Ltd.

Cargill, D. 1841. *Memoirs of Mrs Margaret Cargill, Wife of the Reverend David Cargill, AM, Wesleyan Missionary. Including Notices of the Progress of Christianity in Tonga and Fiji. By Her Husband.* London: John Mason.

Chalmers, J. 1880. "The London Missionary Society and its Native Teachers." *The Brisbane Courier* Wednesday 7 January, 5.

Chalmers, J. and W. W. Gill. 1885. *Work and Adventure in New Guinea: 1877 to 1885.* London: Religious Tract Society.

Christie's. 2013. *Art d'Afrique, d'Océanie et d'Amérique du Nord* (sale 3566), 10 December 2013. Paris: Christie's.

Christopher, C. 1971. *The Complete Book of Doll Making and Collecting.* 2nd edition. New York: Dover.

Clunie, F. 1986. *Yalo i Viti. Shades of Fiji: A Fiji Museum Catalogue.* Suva: The Fiji Museum.

Codrington, R. H. 1891. *The Melanesians: Studies in Their Anthropology and Folklore.* Oxford: Clarendon Press.

Comaroff, J. L. and J. Comaroff. 1991. *Of Revelation and Revolution. Vol. 1, Christianity, Colonialism and Consciousness in South Africa,* Vol. 1. Chicago: University of Chicago Press.

Comaroff, J. L. and J. Comaroff. 1997. *Of Revelation and Revolution. Vol. 2, The Dialectics of Modernity on a South African Frontier.* Chicago: University of Chicago Press.

Corris, P. 1970. "Kwaisulia of Ada Gege: A Strong-man in the Solomon Islands." In *Pacific Islands Portraits,* edited by J. W. Davidson & D. Scarr, 253-66. Canberra: Australian National University Press.

Cox, J. 2008. *The British missionary enterprise since 1700.* London: Routledge.

Craig, B. 1988. *Art and Decoration of Central New Guinea.* Princes Risborough: Shire Publications.

Craik, G. L. 1830. *The New Zealanders.* London: Society for the Diffusion of Useful Knowledge.

Crawford, H. V. and P. J. Beard. 2010. *Letters Home from Richard Burdsall Lyth and Mary Ann Lyth, 1829-1856.* Transcribed in 1981 by C. L. Crawford, K. E. Crawford and H. V. Crawford. 1981 version converted to electronic format by H. V. Crawford and P. J. Beard in 2010.

Crossland, Z. 2013. "Signs of Mission: Material Semeiosis and Nineteenth-century Tswana Architecture." *Signs* 1: 79-113.

Dauncey, H. M. 1913. *Papuan Pictures.* London: London Missionary Society.

David, A., F. Fernandez-Armesto, C. Novi and G. Williams (eds.). 2004. *The Malaspina Expedition 1789-1794: Journal of the Voyage by Alejandro Malaspina, Volume III: Manila to Cadiz.* London: The Hakluyt Society.

Davies, J. [1851] 1961. *An English and Tahitian Dictionary.* LMS Press. Tahiti: Éditions Haere Po.

Davies, P. J. E. 1997. "The Politics of Perpetuation: Trajan's Column and the Art of Commemoration." *American Journal of Archaeology* 101(1): 41-65.

Davison, P. & P. Harries. 1980. "Cotton Weaving in South-east Africa: History and Technology." In *Textiles of Africa,* edited by D. Idiens and K. G. Ponting, 175-92. Bath: The Pasold Research Fund Ltd.

Derrick, R. A. 1946. *A History of Fiji.* Suva: Government Press.

Dutton, T. E. 1985. *Police Motu: Iena Sivarai (Its Story).* Port Moresby: University of Papua New Guinea Press.

Edge-Partington, J. 1890-98. *An Album of the Weapons, Tools, Ornaments, Articles of Dress, etc., of the Natives of the Pacific Islands.* Manchester: Printed Privately.

Edwards, E. 2012. *The camera as historian: amateur photographers and historical imagination, 1885-1918.* Durham, North Carolina: Duke University Press.

Ellis, W. [1831] 1969. *Polynesian Researches.* 4 volumes. Rutland: C. E. Tuttle.

Endfield, G. H. and D. J. Nash. 2007. "'A Good Site for Health': Missionaries and the Pathological Geography of Central Southern Africa." *Singapore Journal of Tropical Geography* 28: 142–57.

Evara, R. A. 2013. "Zurenuoc Banishes 'Ungodly Images and Idols' from Parliament: Speaker 'Cleanses' House." *The Papua New Guinea Post-Courier*, December 6 (accessed July 2014).

Eves, H. and N. Haley. 2014. "Ungodly images and idols: debating national identity in the national parliament." In Purging Parliament: A New Christian Politics in Papua New Guinea? *SSGM Discussion Paper* 1: 1-21. (available online: http://ips.cap.anu.edu.au/ssgm, accessed July 2014).

Eves, H. *et al.* 2014. "Purging Parliament: A New Christian Politics in Papua New Guinea?" *SSGM Discussion Paper* 1: 1-21. (available online: http://ips.cap.anu.edu.au/ssgm, accessed July 2014).

Farnfield, T. 1958a. "Fiji Art Recalls Cannibals." *Toledo Blade* 4 April 1958, 17.

Farnfield, T. 1958b. "Cannibal Day Relics Return to Fiji Island." *Spokane Daily Chronicle* 7 April 1958, 34.

Farnfield, T. 1958c. "Human Bone Needles Top Fiji Trophies." *The Miami News* 28 April 1958, 5.

Fischer, H. 1983[1932]. *Sound-producing instruments in Oceania : construction and playing technique-distribution and function.* Translated by Philip W. Holzknecht; edited by Don Niles. Boroko: Institute of Papua New Guinea Studies.

Fox, C. E. 1924. *The Threshold of the Pacific: An Account of the Social Organisation, Magic and Religion of the People of San Cristoval in the Solomon Islands.* London: Kegan Paul.

Frazer, J. G. 1890. *The Golden Bough: A Study in Comparative Religion.* 2 volumes. New York: MacMillan and Co.

Gardner, H. B. 2006. *Gathering for God: George Brown in Oceania.* Dunedin: Otago University Press.

Garson, J. G. and C. H. Read. 1899. *Notes and Queries on Anthropology, edited for the British Association for the Advancement of Science (Third Edition).* London: The Anthropological Institute.

Gikandi, S. 1998 (ed.), *Uganda's Katikiro in England by Ham Mukasa.* Translated from Luganda by Rev. Ernest Millar. Manchester: Manchester University Press.

Gordon, H. C. 1899. "Lesser Known Museums: The London Missionary Society Museum." *English Illustrated Magazine* XXI: 81-84.

Gosseau, C. 1997. *Le couteau d'exécution et ses dérivés = execution knives & derivatives = executie messen en verwanten = Exekutionsmesser und verwandte Formen.* Brussels: Tribal Arts.

Gravelle, K. 1979. *Fiji's Times: A History of Fiji.* Suva: Fiji Times.

Gunson, N. 1994. "British Missionaries and Their Contribution to Science in the Pacific Islands." In *Darwin's Laboratory: Evolutionary Theory and Natural History in the Pacific*, edited by R. M. MacLeod and P. F. Rehbock, 283-316. Honolulu: University of Hawaii Press.

Haddon, A. C. 1894. *The Decorative Art of British New Guinea: A Study in Papuan Ethnography*. Dublin: Royal Irish Academy.

Haddon, A. C. 1895. *Evolution in Art: As Illustrated by the Life-Histories of Designs*. London: Walter Scott.

Haddon, A. C. 1912. *Reports of the Cambridge Anthropological Expedition to Torres Straits: Arts and Crafts*. Volume IV. Cambridge: Cambridge University Press.

Hadfield, E. 1920. *Among the Natives of the Loyalty Group*. London: Macmillan.

Heath, L. M. 1987. "Matai-ni-mate, Carpenter of Sickness: The Reverend Richard Burdsall Lyth, M.R.C.S., L.S.A., and the Wesleyan Mission in Fiji, a Case-study in Mission Contact Relationships in Pre-Cession Fiji, 1839 to 1854." PhD Thesis. University of Queensland.

Henry, T. 1928. *Ancient Tahiti*. Bishop Museum Bulletin No. 48. Honolulu: Bishop Museum.

Hepburn, Rev. J. D. [1895] 1970. *Twenty Years in Khama's Country*. London: Frank Cass & Co.

Herle, A. and S. Rouse (eds.). 1998. *Cambridge and the Torres Strait: Centenary Essays on the 1898 Anthropological Expedition*. Cambridge: Cambridge University Press.

Hilliard, D. 1978. *God's Gentlemen: A History of the Melanesian Mission 1849–1942*. Brisbane: Queensland University Press.

Hocart, A. M. 1952. *The Northern States of Fiji*. London: Royal Anthropological Institute of Great Britain and Ireland.

Hooper, S. 2006. *Pacific Encounters: Art and Divinity in Polynesia 1760-1860*. London: British Museum Press.

Hooper, S. 2007. "Embodying Divinity: The Life of A'a." In S. Hooper (ed.), *Polynesian Art: Histories and Meanings in Cultural Contexts*. Special issue of the *Journal of the Polynesian Society* 116 (2): 131-80.

Hooper, S. 2008. "La collecte comme iconoclasm: La London Missionary Society en Polynésie." *Gradhiva: Revue d'Anthropologie et de Muséologie* 7: 120-33. Paris: Musée du quai Branly.

Hooper, S. 2014. "A Cross-cultural Theory of Relics: Religion, Bodies, Artefacts, Images and Art." *World Art* 4 (2): 175-207.

Hopkins, A. I. 1928. *In the Isles of King Solomon: An Account of Twenty-five Years Spent amongst the Primitive Solomon Islanders*. London: Seeley, Service & Co.

Hopkins, A. I. 1934. *Autobiography of Fr. Arthur Hopkins*. Church of Melanesia Archives, National Archives, Honiara. Published by Project Canterbury 2005, accessible online at [http://anglicanhistory.org/oceania/aihopkins/ms1934.html].

Hughson, D. 1817. *Walks through London.* London: W. Wilson.

Hunt, C. 1981. *Shark Tooth and Stone Blade: Pacific Island Art from the University of Aberdeen.* Aberdeen: Aberdeen University Press.

Ivens, W. G. 1927. *Melanesians of the South-east Solomon Islands.* London: Kegan Paul.

Ivens, W. G. 1930. *The Island Builders of the Pacific.* London: Seeley, Service & Co.

Jacobs, K. 2012. *Collecting Kamoro: Objects, Encounters and Representation on the southwest coast of Papua.* Mededelingen van het Rijksmuseum voor Volkenkunde 41. Leiden: National Museum of Ethnology and Sidestone Press.

Jacobs, K. 2014. "Inscribing missionary impact in Central Polynesia: mapping the George Bennet collection (1821–1824)." *Journal of the History of Collections* 26(2): 263-276.

Jacobs, K. and C. Wingfield. 2014. "Who cares? The material heritage of British missions in Africa and the Pacific, and its future." *Journal of Museum Ethnography* 27: 129-136.

Jefferson, T. and J. H. Robinson. 1995. "An American Cabinet of Curiosities: Thomas Jefferson's 'Indian Hall at Monticello'." *Winterthur Portfolio* 30(1): 41-58.

Jessop [Nuku], M. 2007. "Unwrapping Gods: Encounters with Gods and Missionaries in Tahiti and the Austral Islands 1797–1830." PhD thesis. Norwich: Sainsbury Research Unit (SRU), University of East Anglia.

Johnston, H. 1908. *George Grenfell and the Congo,* Vol. I. London: Hutchinson.

Johnston, H. H. 1998 [1904]. "Introduction". In *Uganda's Katikiro in England by Ham Mukasa,* edited by S. Gikandi. Manchester: Manchester University Press, pp. 41-46.

Kenseth, J. (ed.) 1991. *The Age of the Marvelous.* Hanover, N.H.: Hood Museum of Art, Dartmouth College.

King, Rev. J. 1909. *W. G. Lawes of Savage Island and New Guinea.* London: The Religious Tract Society.

Kirk, J. 1861-2. "Report on the Natural Products and Capabilities of the Shire and Lower Zambesi Valleys." *Proceedings of the Royal Geographical Society of London,* Vol. 6, No. 1, 25-32. Accessible online at [http://www.jstor.org/stable/1799376]. Accessed 19 July 2013.

Kirshenblatt-Gimblett, B. 1991. "Objects of Ethnography." In *Exhibiting Cultures: The Poetics and Politics of Museum Display,* edited by I. Karp and S. D. Lavine, 386-443. Washington: Smithsonian Institution Press.

Koerner, L. 2004. *The Reformation of the Image.* London: Reaktion Books.

Kwami, A. 2013. *Kumasi Realism, 1951-2007: An African Modernism.* London: Hurst.

Landau, P. S. 1995. *The Realm of the Word: Language, Gender and Christianity in a Southern African Kingdom.* Portsmouth, NH: Heinemann.

Lane, P. J. 1999. "Archaeology, Nonconformist Missions and the 'Colonisation of Consciousness' in Southern Africa, c.1820–1900." In *Case Studies in Archaeology and World Religion,* edited by T. Insoll, 153–65. BAR International Series 755. Oxford: British Archaeological Reports.

Lange, R. 2006. *Island Ministers: Indigenous Leadership in Nineteenth Century Pacific Islands Christianity.* Canberra: Pandanus Books.

Langmore, D. 1989. *Missionary Lives, 1874-1914.* Honolulu: University of Hawaii Press.

Larsson, K. E. 1960. *Fijian Studies.* Etnologiska Studier Volume 25. Göteborg : Etnografiska Museet.

Latour, B. 1993 [1991]. *We Have Never Been Modern.* New York; London: Harvester Wheatsheaf.

Latukefu, S. 1969. "The Case of the Wesleyan Mission in Tonga." *Journal de la Société des Océanistes* 25: 95-112.

Lawes, W. G. 1880. "Notes on New Guinea and Its Inhabitants." *Proceedings of the Royal Geographical Society and Monthly Record of Geography* 2 (10): 602-16.

Lawes, W. G. 1885. *Grammar and Vocabulary of the Language Spoken by the Motu Tribe, New Guinea.* Sydney: Government Printer.

Lawry, W. 1850. *Friendly and Feejee Islands: A Missionary Visit to Various Stations in the South Seas, in the Year MDCCCXLVII.* London: Charles Gilpin.

Lawson, B. 1994. *Collected Curios: Missionary tales from the South Seas.* Fontana Monograph Series 3. Montreal: McGill University.

Leggatt, Rev T. W. 1896. *Agnes C. P. Watt, Twenty-five Years' Mission Life on Tanna, New Hebrides,* Paisley: J. & R. Parlane.

Livingstone, D. 1857. *Missionary Travels and Researches in South Africa.* London: John Murray.

Livingstone, D. and C. Livingstone. 2005. *Narrative of an Expedition to the Zambesi and its Tributaries: And of the Discovery of the Lakes Shirwa and Nyassa.* Stroud: Nonsuch Publishing Ltd. (originally published London: John Murray, 1865).

LMS. 1826. *Catalogue of the Missionary Museum, Austin Friar's, Including Specimens in Natural History ... Idols ... Dresses, etc.* London: Missionary Museum.

LMS. n.d.. *Catalogue of the Missionary Museum, Blomfield Street, Finsbury: Including Specimens in Natural History, Various Idols of Heathen Nations, Dresses, Manufactures, Domestic Utensils, Instruments of War &c....* London: Missionary Museum.

LMS. 1896. *Report of the Directors to the General Meeting of the Missionary Society, Usually Called the London Missionary Society.* London: Printed by Order of the General Meeting.

Lovett, R. 1899. *The History of the London Missionary Society, 1795-1895.* London: Oxford University Press.

Lydon, J. 2005. *Eye Contact.* London: Duke University Press.

MacClancy, J. 1988. "A Natural Curiosity, the British Market for Primitive Art, Anthropology and Aesthetics." *Res* 15: 163-176.

Mackenzie, J. 1871. *Ten Years North of the Orange River: A Story of Everyday Life and Work among the South African Tribes from 1859 to 1869.* London: Edmonston and Douglas.

MacMillan, A. T. 1999. "Introduction, Communion Tokens". In *Communion Tokens of the World,* L. M. Burzinski. Madison: Straus Printing Co.

Mathers, E. P. 1895. *Zambezia: England's El Dorado in Africa*. London: King, Sell & Railton.

Mayer, C. E. 2009. "A Reconciliation Ceremony on Erromango: Not a Story about Cannibalism." *Tok Blong Pasifik* 7 (2): 7-11.

Mayer, C. E., A. Naupa and V. Warri. 2013. *No Longer Captives of the Past: The Story of a Reconciliation Ceremony on Erromango*. Vancouver and Port Vila: UBC Museum of Anthropology and Erromango Cultural Society.

McFarlane, S. 1888. *Among the Cannibals of New Guinea: Being the Story of the New Guinea Mission of the London Missionary Society*. London: London Missionary Society.

Mearns, B. and R. Mearns. 1998. *The Bird Collectors*. New York: Academic Press.

Mgadla, P. 1986. "Missionary and Colonial Education among the Bangwato, 1862-1948." PhD thesis. Boston University.

Miller, D. E., K. H. Sargeant and R. Flory (eds.). 2013. *Spirit and Power: The Growth and Global Impact of Pentecostalism*. Oxford: Oxford University Press.

Moffat, J. S. 1890. *The Lives of Robert and Mary Moffat*. 12th ed. London: T. Fisher Unwin.

Moffat, R. 1842. *Missionary Labours and Scenes in Southern Africa*. London: John Snow.

Moore, C. and S. Mullins (eds.). 2012. "Andrew Goldie's Memoir: 1875-1879." *Memoirs of the Queensland Museum – Culture* 6: 39-127.

Morton, C. 2004. "Fixity and Fluidity: Chiefly Authority and Settlement Movement in Colonial Botswana." *History and Anthropology* 15: 345–65.

Mullen, S. 2012. "One of Scotia's 'Sons of Toil': David Livingstone and Blantyre Mill." In *David Livingstone. Man, Myth and Legacy*, edited by S. Worden, 15-31. Edinburgh: NMSE Enterprises Ltd.

Mullins, S. and D. Wetherall. 1996. "LMS Teachers in Torres Strait and New Guinea." In *The Covenant Makers: Islander Missionaries in the Pacific*, edited by D. Munro and A. Thornley, 186-209. Suva, Fiji: Pacific Islands Theological College and the Institute of Pacific Studies at the University of the South Pacific.

Mundus Gateway. "Mundus: Gateway to missionary collections in the UK." Accessible online at [www.mundus.ac.uk].

Munro, D. & A. Thornley (eds.). 1996. *The Covenant Makers: Islander Missionaries in the Pacific*. Suva: Pacific Theological College.

Neich, R. 2007. "From Goddesses to Missionary Trophies to Masterpieces." *Journal of the Polynesian Society* 116 (2): 213-68.

Newbury, C. 1967. "*Te Hau Pahu Rahi:* Pomare II and the Concept of Inter-island Government in Eastern Polynesia." *Journal of the Polynesian Society* 76: 477-514.

Northcott, C. 1945. *Glorious Company: One Hundred and Fifty Years Life and Work of the London Missionary Society 1795-1945*. London: Livingstone Press.

Northcott, C. 1965. *South Seas Sailor: The Story of John Williams and His Ships*. London: Lutterworth Press.

Parkinson, R. [1907] 1999. *Thirty Years in the South Seas: Land and People, Customs and Traditions in the Bismarck Archipelago and on the German Solomon Islands.* Transl. by J. Dennison, edited by B. Ankermann. Honolulu: University of Hawaii Press.

Parsons, Q.N. 1973. "Khama III, the Bamangwato and the British - with Special Reference to 1895-1923." PhD thesis. University of London.

Parsons, Q.N. 1998. *King Khama, Emperor Joe, and the Great White Queen.* Oxford: James Currey.

Paton, M. W. 1905. *Letters and Sketches from the New Hebrides.* London: Hodder & Stoughton.

Paton, Rev. J. (ed.) 1911. *The Story of John G. Paton, Told for Young Folks.* London: Hodder & Stoughton.

Patterson, Rev. G. 1882. *Missionary Life among the Cannibals, Being the Life of Rev. John Geddie, First Missionary to the New Hebrides, with A History of the Nova Scotia Presbyterian Mission on that Group.* Toronto: James Campbell & Son.

Philp, J. [*in press,* 2014]. "Krar: 19th-Century Turtle-shell Masks from Mabuyag Collected by Samuel McFarlane." *Memoirs of the Queensland Museum.*

Powerhouse Museum. [n.d.]. "H4686 Ship model, SS 'John Williams IV', London Missionary Society steamer." *Powerhouse Museum Collection Search 2.53.* Accessible online at [http://www.powerhousemuseum.com/collection/database/?irn=240492].

Ramsay, E. P. 1877. "Note of a Species of Echidna (Tachyglossus), from Port Moresby, New Guinea." *Proceedings of the Linnean Society of New South Wales* 2: 31-3.

Ready, J. L. 1985. *Forgotten Allies: the Military Contribution of the Colonies, Exiled Governments, and Lesser Powers to the Allied Victory in World War II.* Jefferson, NC: Mcfarland.

Reid, A., P. J. Lane, A. K. Segobye, L. Börjeson, N. Mathibidi and P. Sekgarametso. 1997. "Tswana Architecture and Responses to Colonialism." *World Archaeology* 28: 370–92.

Robertson H. A. 1903. *Erromanga: The Martyr Isle.* London, Hodder & Stoughton.

Robinson, D., S. Herbert and R. Crangle. 2001 (eds.). *Encyclopaedia of the Magic Lantern.* London: Magic Lantern Society.

Roscoe, J. 1907. "Kibuka, the War God of the Baganda." *Man* 7: 161-6.

Roscoe, J. 1911. *The Baganda: An Account of their Native Customs and Beliefs.* London: MacMillan and Co.

Ross. R. M. 1983. *Melanesians at Mission Bay: A History of the Melanesian Mission.* Wellington: New Zealand Historic Places Trust.

Ross, A. C. 2002. *David Livingstone: Mission and Empire.* London: Hambledon Continuum.

Schapera, I. (ed.) 1951. *Apprenticeship at Kuruman: Being the Journals and Letters of Robert and Mary Moffat 1820-1828.* London: Chatto & Windus.

Schoeman, K. 1995. *A Thorn Bush that Grows in the Path: The Missionary Career of Ann Hamilton, 1815-1823.* Cape Town: South African Library.

Schram, R. 2014. *A New Government breaks with the Past in The Papua New Guinea Parliament's "Haus Tambaran"*. Material World Blog posted 9 February 2014. (available online: http://www.materialworldblog.com/2014/02/a-new-government-breaks-with-the-past-in-the-papua-new-guinea-parliaments-haus-tambaran/, accessed July 2014).

Sclater, P. L. 1893. "The Bird-Collections in the Oxford University Museum (Letters, Extracts, Notices)." *Ibis* 35 (1): 156-7.

Seton, R. 2012. "Reconstructing the Museum of the *London Missionary Society." Material Religion* 8 (1): 98-102.

Sharpe, B. R. 1877/79 "Contributions to the Ornithology of New Guinea.—Part VI. On Collections Made by the Rev. W. G. Lawes in South-eastern New Guinea." *Journal of the Linnean Society of London* 14 (79): 685–8.

Sivasundaram, S. 2005. *Nature and the Godly Empire: Science and Evangelical Mission in the Pacific, 1795-1850.* Cambridge: Cambridge University Press.

Smith, D. 2010. "'We Wia Waga': Missionary Collections and Synergetic Assemblages in the Solomon Islands 1920-1942." *International Journal of Historical Archaeology* 14: 188-208.

Smith, K. 1920. *Congoland: A Book for Young People.* London: Carey Press.

Smith, V. and N. Thomas (eds.). 2013. *Mutiny and Aftermath: James Morrison's Account of the Mutiny on the Bounty and the Island of Tahiti.* Honolulu: University of Hawaii Press.

Speiser, F. 1996 [1923]. *Ethnology of Vanuatu: an early twentieth century study.* Honolulu: University of Hawaii Press.

Spieth, J. [2008] 2011. *The Ewe People [Die Ewe-Stamme].* Accra: Sub-Saharan Publishers.

Squires, N. 2003. "Fijians Killed and Ate a Missionary in 1867. Yesterday Their Descendants Apologised." *UK Telegraph* 14 November 2003. Accessible online at [http://www.telegraph.co.uk/news/worldnews/australiaandthepacific/fiji/1446723/Fijians-killed-and-ate-a-missionary-in-1867.-Yesterday-their-descendants-apologised.html]. Accessed 9 June 2013.

Stanley, N. 1989. "The Unstable Object: Reviewing the Status of Ethnographic Artifacts." *Journal of Design History* 2.2 (3): 108-21.

Stanley, N. 1994. "Recording Island Melanesia: The Significance of the Melanesian Mission in Museum Records." *Pacific Arts* 9 (10): 25-41.

Steel, R. 1880. *The New Hebrides and Christian Missions, with a Sketch of the Labour Traffic, and Notes of a Cruise through the Group on a Mission Vessel.* London: James Nisbet & Co.

Steyn, G. 2011. "The Spatial Patterns of Tswana Stone-walled Towns in Perspective." *South African Journal of Art History* 26 (2): 101-25.

Sutton Smith, H. C. 1911. *Yakusu, the Very Heart of Africa: Being Some Account of the Protestant Mission at Stanley Falls, Upper Congo.* London: Marshall Brothers Ltd.

Thompson, T. J. 2012. *Light on Darkness? Missionary Photography of Africa in the Nineteenth and Early Twentieth Centuries.* Grand Rapids, Michigan: William B Eerdmans.

Thomson, B. 1894. *The Diversions of a Prime Minister.* London: Blackwood.

Tomlinson, M. 2012. "Passports to Eternity: Whales' Teeth and Transcendence in Fijian Methodism." In *Flows of Religious Faith: Religious Reach and Community in Asia and the Pacific,* edited by L. Manderson, W. Smith and M. Tomlinson, 215-31. Dordrecht: Springer.

Toren, C. 1995. "Seeing the Ancestral Sites: Transformations in Fijian Notions of the Land." In *The Anthropology of Landscape: Perspectives on Place and Space,* edited by E. Hirsch and M. O'Hanlon, 163-83. Oxford: Clarendon Press.

Tristram, H. B. 1876. "Notes on a Collection of Birds from the New Hebrides." *Ibis* 18 (2): 259–67.

Tristram, H. B. 1889. *Catalogue of a Collection of Birds Belonging to H. B. Tristram, D.D., F.R.S.* Durham: Advertiser.

Tucker, C. 1836. "Extracts from a Letter Written at Ha'apai, March 12th-September 30th 1835." *Methodist Missionary Society Notices* 242.

Urbanowicz, C. F. 1977. "Motives and Methods: Missionaries in Tonga in the Early 19th Century." *Journal of the Polynesian Society* 86 (2): 245-63.

Van der Grijp, P. 2002. "Travelling Gods and Nasty Spirits: Ancient Religious Representations and Missionization in Tonga (Polynesia)." *Paideuma* 48: 243-60.

Walton, J. 1956. *African Village.* Pretoria: J. L. van Schaik Ltd.

Warren, S. 1827. *Chronicles of Wesleyan Methodism: A Digest of all Its Laws and Regulations with a Comprehensive Statement of Its Principal Doctrines.* Volume 1. London: John Stephens.

Webb, V. L. 1998. "Missionary Photographers in the Pacific Islands; Divine Light." *History of Photography* 21 (1): 12-22.

Webb, V. L. 2006. "In Situ: Photographs of Art in the Papuan Gulf." In *Coaxing the Spirits to Dance: Art and Society in the Papuan Gulf of New Guinea,* edited by R. L. Welsch, V. L. Webb, and S. Haraha, 52-79. New Hanover: Hood Museum of Art and Dartmouth College.

Wench, I. 1961. *Mission to Melanesia.* London: Elek Books.

Wesley, F. 2008. "So What Really Happened?" *Fiji Times* 28 September 2008. Accessible online at [http://www.fijitimes.com/satory.aspx?id=102178]. Accessed 2 October 2013.

Wilkes, C. 1845. *Narrative of the United States Exploring Expedition during the Years 1838, 1839, 1840, 1841, 1842.* Volume 3. Philadelphia: Lea & Blanchard.

Williams, J. 1837. *A Narrative of Missionary Enterprises in the South Sea Islands: With Remarks upon the Natural History of the Islands, Origin, Languages, Traditions, and Usages of the Inhabitants.* 1st Edition. London: J. Snow.

Williams, J. 1841. *A Narrative of Missionary Enterprises in the South Sea Islands: With Remarks upon the Natural History of the Islands, Origin, Languages, Traditions, and Usages of the Inhabitants.* 2nd Edition. London: J. Snow.

Williams, T. 1858. *Fiji and the Fijians. Volume I, The Islands and Their Inhabitants.* Edited by G. S. Rowe. London: Heylin.

Williams, T. 1931. *The Journal of Thomas Williams, Missionary in Fiji, 1840-1853*. 2 vols. Edited by G. C. Henderson. Sydney: Angus & Robertson.

Willoughby, W. C. 1900. *Native Life on the Transvaal Border*. London: Simpkin, Marshall, Hamilton, Kent & Co.

Wilson, G. 1858. "Annual Report of the Director of the Industrial Museum of Scotland 1856, Appendix C to the 4th Report of Department of Science and Art, Industrial Museum, Scotland". In *Directory of the Industrial Museum of Scotland and of the Natural History Museum Edinburgh*, 161-70. London: Chapman & Hall.

Wingfield, C. 2012a. "The Moving Objects of the London Missionary Society: An Experiment in Symmetrical Anthropology." PhD thesis, submitted to the College of Arts and Law. Birmingham: University of Birmingham.

Wingfield, Chris. 2012b. "Remembering David Livingstone 1873-1935: From Celebrity to Saintliness." In *David Livingstone: the Man, the Myth and the Legacy*, edited by S. Worden, 115-129. Edinburgh: National Museums Scotland Press.

Wood, A. H. 1978. *Overseas Missions of the Australian Methodist Church, Volume Two: Fiji*. Melbourne: Aldersgate Press.

Notes on Contributors

Adams, Julie studied at the Sainsbury Research Unit for the Arts of Africa, Oceania and the Americas. Her PhD examined the significance of Maori cloaks in contemporary Maori art. She has worked on major research and exhibition projects at the British Museum, National Museums Scotland and the Museum of Archaeology and Anthropology, Cambridge. She is currently Senior Research Associate on the European Research Council-funded project *Pacific Presences: Oceanic Art and European Museums*. The project investigates the extensive Pacific holdings of a series of European institutions in a bid to further advance understandings of materiality and cross-cultural histories, as well as present-day museum policy and practice.

Ashley, Ceri is a Senior Lecturer in Archaeology at the University of Pretoria, and directed the excavations of the Lake Ngami mission in the Khwebe Hills in 2008 and 2009. She has previously held research positions at UCLA and UCL Institute of Archaeology, and has conducted archaeological research in Kenya, Uganda, South Africa and Botswana.

Bell, Joshua, a cultural anthropologist, is currently Curator of Globalization at the Smithsonian Institution's National Museum of Natural History and Director of the Recovering Voices Program. Combining ethnographic fieldwork with research in museums and archives, he examines the shifting local and global network of relationships between persons, artefacts and the environment. His publications address these topics in relation to his ongoing research with communities of the Purari Delta of Papua New Guinea, histories of collecting and collections from the Pacific and new research on the meanings and uses of mobile phones.

Buadromo, Sagale has been the Director of the Fiji Museum since 2001, having begun work at the Fiji Museum in 1989. She is very interested in the motifs and designs used in *masi* (barkcloth) making and is interested in examining old examples of *masi* (pre-1850) in museum collections abroad and comparing them to the contemporary designs currently being used by *masi* makers in Fiji today.

Burt, Ben, a curator in the Department of Africa, Oceania and Americas at the British Museum, is an anthropologist who has researched with the Kwara'ae people of Malaita since 1979. He has published studies of colonialism and Christianity, land tenure, forest resources and material culture, history and art, in collaboration with Michael Kwa'ioloa.

Cadbury, Tabitha is a Curator of Social History and World Cultures at the Plymouth City Museum and Art Gallery. She studied Archaeology and Anthropology at the University of Cambridge, the Arts of Africa, Oceania and the Americas at the University of East Anglia, and Heritage Management at Nottingham Trent University. She is also an Associate Member of the Museums

Association. She has managed, researched and curated ethnography, folklore and local history collections for over twenty years, at a number of institutions including the Museum of Mankind, the Cambridge University Museum of Archaeology and Anthropology, and the Royal Albert Memorial Museum in Exeter. She is currently a doctoral student in Historical Studies at Bristol University, researching English material magic in museums.

Charles-Rault, Jacqueline graduated from Falmouth School of Art in Cornwall, England, in 1987. She has been living in France for the past twenty-five years, where she is currently the Director of the Cultural Service at the University of Le Havre and teaches English as a foreign language to science students at the University. Over the past ten years she has researched contemporary Maori and Pacific art, with added emphasis on Maori women artists, having visited and lived in New Zealand for a short period of time. She has curated two contemporary exhibitions and is currently preparing an exhibition of contemporary Pacific art to be held in France in 2015.

Dudding, Jocelyne is the Manager of Photograph Collections at the Museum of Archaeology and Anthropology, University of Cambridge. Her research focuses on photographs as objects of cultural property, and she has worked with a number of originating communities to access their related imagery in the Museum's Photograph Collections.

Elliott, Catherine Weinberg is currently undertaking doctoral studies at the University of East Anglia, writing a thesis on the South Africa collection at the British Museum. Until recently a Museum Assistant within the Africa section of the Department of Africa, Oceania and the Americas at the British Museum, she holds a Master's degree in Museum Studies from University College London. She previously worked with mainly African art in Johannesburg and London following her studies at the University of the Witwatersrand, Johannesburg.

Haddow, Eve is Assistant Curator in the Department of World Cultures at National Museums Scotland, responsible for a project funded by Esmée Fairbairn Collections Fund to review Pacific collections in Scottish museums. The project is a partnership between Aberdeen University Museums, Glasgow Museums, Perth Museum and Art Gallery and National Museums Scotland. She studied Social Anthropology at the University of Edinburgh prior to completing an MA in Art Gallery and Museum Studies at the University of Manchester. She worked and volunteered in several museum collections roles prior to embarking on the Pacific Collections Review in April 2013.

Hand, Rachel is the Collections Manager for Anthropology at the Museum of Archaeology and Anthropology, University of Cambridge. Her research interests and publications include Irish collecting within the context of the British Empire and the North American and Pacific collections from the voyages of Captain James Cook held at the National Museum of Ireland, Dublin.

Hasell, Jill is Museum Assistant for the Oceania section of The British Museum. She is responsible for the day-to-day care of the Pacific and Australian collections. Her work includes the supervision of research visits, documentation and exhibition-related duties. She has researched aspects of the history of the collection and its collectors.

Herle, Anita is Senior Curator for Anthropology at the University of Cambridge Museum of Archaeology and Anthropology, where she has particular responsibility for collections from the Pacific and the Americas. She has regional interests in Torres Strait, Vanuatu, Fiji and Canada. Her research areas include museum anthropology, the early history of British anthropology, art and aesthetics, and visual histories. She coordinates an MPhil course in Social Anthropology and Museums and teaches in museology, the anthropology of art and visual media.

Hooper, Steven is Director of the Sainsbury Research Unit for the Arts of Africa, Oceania and the Americas and Professor of Visual Arts at the University of East Anglia. He received his PhD in Social Anthropology from the University of Cambridge, having conducted over two years of fieldwork in Fiji. He has recently directed AHRC-funded research projects focusing on Polynesian and Fijian art, leading to the exhibition and book *Pacific Encounters: Art and Divinity in Polynesia 1760–1860* (2006) and to current work on an exhibition and book on Fijian art. Among his interests is the history of collecting, and he has published on missionary collecting in the Pacific. He is President of the Pacific Arts Association.

Igglesden, Katrina Talei is a PhD candidate at the Sainbury Research Unit for the Arts of Africa, Oceania & the Americas. She is conducting her doctoral research on the changing social biography of *masi* (Fijian barkcloth) when used in contemporary contexts, both in Fiji and by Fijians abroad. A member of the large and dynamic diasporic Fijian communities of both London (United Kingdom) and Vancouver (Canada), she is interested in how traditional *masi* manufacture and presentation processes are emulated in culturally driven arenas such as the rapidly expanding "high fashion" scene.

Jacobs, Karen is Lecturer in the Arts of the Pacific at the Sainsbury Research Unit for the Arts of Africa, Oceania and the Americas, University of East Anglia, Norwich. She is interested in aspects of collecting and the history of collections, cultural festivals, the politics of clothing, and contemporary Pacific art. She has published on and has been involved in research and exhibition projects on Fiji, Polynesia and the Kamoro region in West Papua – the latter culminating in her book *Collecting Kamoro* (2012).

Knowles, Chantal is currently Head of Cultural Environments Program at Queensland Museum, Brisbane. Prior to this, she spent thirteen years at National Museums Scotland, Edinburgh as Principal Curator for Oceania, Americas and Africa. She was Chair of the Museum Ethnographers Group, 2011-2014.

Lane, Paul is Professor of Global Archaeology at Uppsala University and co-ordinator of the Resilience in East African Landscapes (REAL) Marie Curie Initial Training Network. He is an archaeologist with over twenty-five years' research experience in Africa. His main research interests are in the organisation and use of space and time in pre-industrial societies, the historical ecology of African landscapes, the archaeology of colonial encounters, cultural perceptions of place, the materialisation of memory, maritime archaeology and the transition to farming in Africa. His doctoral research (1980–1986) at Cambridge University was an ethno-archaeological study of space and time among the Dogon in Mali, West Africa. Before joining Uppsala University, he taught archaeology at the University of Dar es Salaam (1989–1991), University of Botswana (1992–1997) and the University of York (2007–2013). He also served as director of the British Institute in Eastern Africa, Nairobi, from 1998 to 2006. His recent publications include the *Oxford Handbook of African Archaeology* (2013) co-edited with Peter Mitchell, and *Slavery in Africa: Archaeology and Memory* (2011) co-edited with Kevin MacDonald.

Mayer, Carol E. is head of the curatorial department at the UBC Museum of Anthropology (MOA), where she is responsible for the Oceanic and African collections. Her regional interests include Fiji, Vanuatu, Papua New Guinea and, more recently, New Zealand. Her current research interests are the history of Pacific Islands' collections in Canada, the exploration of intellectual property rights, and the building of collaborative networks between the Pacific and the Northwest Coast. In 2013 she organised the PAA International symposium in Vancouver, Canada, curated the exhibition *Paradise Lost? Contemporary Arts of the Pacific* and authored (with Anna Naupa and Vanessa Warri) the book *No Longer Captives of the Past: The Story of a Reconciliation Ceremony on Erromango*.

Mills, Andy is an anthropologist, cultural historian, museum professional and researcher. He specialises in the study of wood sculpture from 18th- and 19th-century Western Polynesia, within the context of broader interests in violent conflict, pre-Christian religion, identity, the body and material style. He has worked as a researcher or curator for a number of museums and universities across the UK, and is currently a research associate on the Fijian Art project in the Sainsbury Research Unit for the Arts of Africa, Oceania and the Americas at the University of East Anglia.

Nuku, Maia is the Evelyn A. J. Hall and John A. Friede Associate Curator for Oceanic Art in the Department of the Arts of Africa, Oceania, and the Americas at the Metropolitan Museum of Art. She previously worked as Research Associate on the European Research Council-funded project *Pacific Presences: Oceanic Art and European Museums*. Her doctoral thesis, "Unwrapping Gods: Encounters with Gods and Missionaries in Tahiti & the Austral Islands 1797–1830" (Sainsbury Research Unit, 2007), focused on early missionary collections of wrapped and bound god images and her ongoing research is grounded in drawing out the often eclipsed cosmological aspects of artefacts, which have tended to be lost in the historical and museological record.

Semu, Greg is an independent researcher, curator and artist who has exhibited his work globally. Born in New Zealand, Greg Semu embraces Samoa as his ancestral and spiritual home. His Samoan *Tatau* has featured in his artwork: 1995 triptych and 2012 triptych commissioned by the Auckland Art Gallery. In 2007, Semu was awarded the inaugural artist in residence position at the Museé du quai Branly, Paris and created *The Battle of the Noble Savage* series. In 2010, the Tjibaou Cultural Centre in New Caledonia commissioned Semu to create *The Last Cannibal Supper, 'Cause Tomorrow We Become Christians,* a politically and historically significant work that explores the dictatorship of Christianity onto "primitive" tribes. Also in 2010, Semu participated in the *Body on the Line, Cultural Warriors* exhibition at the Casula Powerhouse. In 2012, Greg Semu's works were featured in the *Seventh Asia Pacific Triennial of Contemporary Art (APT7)* held at the Queensland Art Gallery. In 2013, he was the winner of the People's Choice Award for the 62nd Blake Prize, with his video installation *Te Upoko o Hoani te Kaiiriiri, The Head of John the Baptist,* 2013. In 2014, Greg Semu was awarded the prestigious Creative New Zealand Visual Arts Residency at the Kunstlerhaus Bethanien, Berlin 2014–2015. Also in 2014, Greg Semu's work featured at the *Melbourne Art Fair*. Greg Semu has lived in Sydney, Australia since 2009. In 2013 he joined the stable of artists at Alcaston Gallery, Melbourne.

Stanley, Nick is an Honorary Research Fellow in the Centre for Anthropology at the British Museum and an Emeritus Professor at Birmingham City University. His most recent book is *The Making of Asmat Art: Indigenous Art in a World Perspective* (Sean Kingston Publishing, 2012).

Thompson, Jack T. is a historian of African Christianity with a special interest in Malawi. He taught for fifteen years at the School of Divinity, University of Edinburgh, where he was Director of the Centre for the Study of World Christianity. He has also been a Visiting Research Fellow at Yale University and a Visiting Professor at Dartmouth College. He retired in 2008, and in 2011–2012 he was Vice Chancellor of the University of Livingstonia in Malawi. He is the author of several books, including *Christianity in Northern Malawi* (1995); *Touching the Heart: Xhosa Missionaries to Malawi* (2000); *Ngoni, Xhosa and Scot: Religious and Cultural Interaction in Malawi* (2007); and *Light on darkness? Missionary Photography of Africa in the Nineteenth and Early Twentieth Centuries* (2012).

Wadra, François is a Kanak archaeologist who has worked in Papua New Guinea, Solomon Islands, Vanuatu and New Caledonia. He is employed by the Provincial Government of the Loyalty Islands to survey significant archaeological sites. He is also a research collaborator on the European Research Council-funded project *Pacific Presences: Oceanic Art and European Museums* (2013–2018) which is based at the Museum of Archaeology and Anthropology, University of Cambridge.

Wate, Ben is a lecturer of Theology & Anthropology at Bishop Patteson theological College, Guadalcanal Solomon Islands. He also worked as Coordinator of Theological Education Review of the Anglican Church of Melanesia based in Honiara Solomon Islands. He received his Bachelor's Degree in Divinity with major in Theology and Ethics from Pacific Theological College, Suva Fiji in 2004. After serving the Anglican Church of Melanesia as Rector of All Saints Parish in Honiara, Ben took up a postgraduate scholarship and studied at the London School of Economics and graduated with a Master of Science in Social Anthropology (MSc) in 2009. While in London, Ben was elected executive member of the Pacific Island Society in UK and Ireland (PISUKI). He is one of the contributors of the book *Melanesia: Art and Encounter* (Bolton *et al.* 2013). Ben is an ordained minister of the Anglican Church of Melanesia. He is currently doing research studies at the University of Otago in New Zealand.

Wingfield, Chris is Senior Curator (Archaeology) at the Museum of Archaeology & Anthropology, University of Cambridge. He has a particular interest in the museum and collections of the London Missionary Society. He has previously worked on a number of research projects at the Pitt Rivers Museum in Oxford and as a curator at Birmingham Museum & Art Gallery.

Worden, Sarah is curator of the African collections at National Museums Scotland (NMS) with particular interest in the cultural significance of African textiles. She was curator of the special bi-centenary exhibition *Dr Livingstone, I Presume* at NMS in 2012–2013 and editor of the 2012 publication *David Livingstone: Man, Myth and Legacy*. She has been working in partnership with Museums of Malawi since 2009, and is co-curator of the 2013 Livingstone bi-centenary exhibition at Chichiri Museum, Blantyre, Malawi.

Zetterstrom-Sharp, Johanna is a Teaching Fellow in Museum Studies at University College London and Assistant Curator of Anthropology at the Horniman Museum and Gardens, with a focus on the African collections. Her research focuses on the intersections between culture, development and transformation in Sierra Leone, and more recently encounters between West African Pentecostal/Charismatic Christian modernity and heritage discourse.

Index of Names and Institutions